Contemporary Architect's Concept Series 29

Fuminori Nousaku: Edifice of the Wild

JN077074

LIXIL Publishing

Contemporary Architect's Concept Series 29
Fuminori Nousaku: Edifice of the Wild

First published in Japan on February 15, 2021 by LIXIL Publishing.

LIXIL Publishing
2-1-1 Ohjima, Koto-ku, Tokyo 136-8535, Japan
TEL: +81 03 3638 8021   FAX: +81 03 3638 8022
https://livingculture.lixil.com/en/publish/

Author: Fuminori Nousaku
Publisher: Jin Song Montesano
Planning and Editing: Jiro Iio,
Mutsumi Nakamura (Speelplaats Co., Ltd.)
Text Translation: Christopher Stephens
Design: Yoshihisa Tanaka, Yutaro Yamada
Series Design: MATCH and Company Co., Ltd.
Printing: Kato Bunmeisha Co., Ltd.

2021 Printed in Japan ISBN978-4-86480-052-5 C0352

現代建築家コンセプト・シリーズ 29

能作文徳 │ 野生のエディフィス

LIXIL出版

Contents

Credits

- 表紙：《西大井のあな》 撮影＝Gottingham
- 裏表紙：《西大井のあな》 撮影＝歌津亮悟
- pp.007‑011：《西大井のあな》 撮影＝Gottingham
  "Untitled (Or the Time That Emerges #88, 153, 187, 236)", 2020 © Gottingham
  Image courtesy of Yoshihisa Tanaka and Studio Xxingham
- pp.012‑013：《Cosmo-Eggs》 撮影＝アーカイ美味んぐ
  提供＝国際交流基金
- pp.014‑015：《ホールのある住宅》 撮影＝新建築社写真部
- pp.016‑017：《ピアノ室のある長屋》 撮影＝鈴木淳平
- pp.018‑019：《Steel House》 撮影＝新建築社写真部
- p.020：《Steel House》 撮影＝Manuel Oka
- p.021：《馬込の平入》 撮影＝鈴木淳平
- p.022：《高岡のゲストハウス》 撮影＝鈴木淳平
- p.023：《高岡のゲストハウス》 撮影＝鈴木淳平
- pp.024‑025：《明野の高床》 撮影＝鈴木淳平
- pp.026‑027：《Bamboo Theater》 撮影＝能作文徳建築設計事務所

- Cover: Holes in the House (Casa a Nishioi)   Photo by Gottingham
- Back cover: Holes in the House (Casa a Nishioi)   Photo by Ryogo Utatsu
- pp.007‑011: Holes in the House (Casa a Nishioi)   Photo by Gottingham
  "Untitled (Or the Time That Emerges #88, 153, 187, 236)", 2020 © Gottingham
  Image courtesy of Yoshihisa Tanaka and Studio Xxingham
- pp.012‑013: Cosmo-Eggs   Photo by ArchiBIMIng
  Courtesy of the Japan Foundation
- pp.014‑015: House with Hall   Photo by Shinkenchiku-sha
- pp.016‑017: Row House with Piano Room   Photo by Jumpei Suzuki
- pp.018‑019: Steel House   Photo by Shinkenchiku-sha
- p.020: Steel House   Photo by Manuel Oka
- p.021: Hirairi in Magome   Photo by Jumpei Suzuki
- p.022: Takaoka Guest House   Photo by Jumpei Suzuki
- p.023: Takaoka Guest House   Photo by Jumpei Suzuki
- pp.024‑025: Akeno Raised-Floor House   Photo by Jumpei Suzuki
- pp.026‑027: Bamboo Theater   Photo by Fuminori Nousaku Architects

精緻な雑種
——事物連関を追い、組み替え、繋ぎ直す

スーパーマーケットの精肉売り場で、奇妙な感覚に囚われた。ふとドキュメンタリー映画のシーン[1]を思い出したのだ。大量の鶏が暗いシェルターに押し込められ、感染症を防ぐためのワクチンが注射されている。過度に栄養を与えられた鶏は自分の体重を支えきれないほど太り、立ち上がってはまた座り込んでいる。鶏の死骸がモモ肉、ムネ肉、ササミなどの部位に分類され、ラップで包装されて綺麗に陳列される。しかし私がいるスーパーマーケットでは動植物の生命の気配は取り除かれ、食品という記号が並んでいる。人間のためにクリーンに整備された人為的な環境にいると、人間だけが世界に存在しているように感じてくる。

　人間が生み出したシステムが巨大になりすぎた世界に私たちは生きている。人間の活動の蓄積が惑星規模のインパクトを持ち始め、地球は安定した気候状態から逸脱し、人新世と呼ばれる暑くて汚染された状態へ移行している[2]。東日本大震災や福島第一原発事故、気候変動による台風や豪雨、感染症などの事象によって人為的な世界が制御不能に陥っている[3]。こうした脆弱な状況のなかで私たちは生きる場所を構築しなければならない。

温暖化などの気候変動の原因は、石油や石炭などの化石燃料の使用による二酸化炭素等の温室効果ガスの排出量の増加であると指摘されている。そのため建築の分野では建設時と使用時のエネルギー消費量や二酸化炭素の排出量の削減は緊急の課題であることは間違いない。しかし「サステイナブル」という考え方には注意が必要である。建設業の関心はいかに持続可能な方法で「建てる」かにあり、建設すること自体に疑問を投げかけるものではない。省エネやCO_2削減自体は批判されることではないが、すでに問題を引き起こしたシステムの内部でそれらは実践されるにすぎず、むしろ既存のシステムを正当化する危険性

すらある[4]。効率性に従属する建築の考え方のなかでは計測された数値だけが価値を持ち、個々の感覚的な経験や創造力は軽視あるいは無視される[5]。エコロジーとは生物と環境の相互作用システムのことであり、そこにはさまざまな生命の生産・消費・分解の営みがある。エコロジーは多様な生命と人工物がいかなるかたちでともに存在するかという根源的な問いである。生態系を構成する諸要素とその関係は非常に複雑であるため、効率化による一元的な解決法ではなく、人間以外の存在とのさまざまな関わり合い、そこから見出されるエコロジカルな生活、それらを柔軟に受け入れる生態学的な感受性が求められるはずである。私が描きたいのは、科学技術のイノベーションによって問題が解決するという楽観的な未来像ではなく、かといって現実の問題を超越した建築の美学でもない。サステイナブルというクリーンな響きとは程遠い、腐敗して朽ち果てていく状態を受け入れ、どうにかやっていくなかで現れる生成的な建築のヴィジョンなのである。

建築は一種の技術である。建設の技術であり、生活の技術である。設計者のデザインした人工物は、人々の行為や経験に対して媒介的な役割を果たしている[6]。それは生活の質を一義的に決定はしないが、生活にいくらか介入する。科学技術と社会を巡って2つの異なる立場がある。社会は科学技術によって規定されるとした技術決定論は、科学的知識や技術は社会から独立していると主張する。これに対し、社会構築主義は科学や技術の探求もまた社会的活動であり、あらゆる知識は社会によって構築されているとした。この2つの間の激しい論争[7]に対して、科学技術を自然か社会かのどちらかに還元しようとする思考そのものに疑問を投げかけたのが、ブルーノ・ラトゥールらのアクターネットワーク論[8]である。アクターネットワーク論では、事物の連関をアクター（行為者）に従って丹念に辿ることによりさまざまな事象が分析される。アクターは人間に限らない。非人間であれ、ほかの事物に変化を与えるものはアクターとみなされる。人間と非人間は相互に独立しておらず、それらの異種混交のネットワークに結びつけられることにより存在様態が変化さ

せられるのである。例えば、新型コロナウイルスの感染拡大の影響で遠隔会議システムZoomの利用者が増えている。Zoomと人間という異質な存在が結びつくことにより、「Zoom人間」という新たなハイブリッドが生成する。それは例えば、在宅ワークで家事と育児をこなす会社員、オンライン演奏会、Zoom飲み、YouTuberのような人気の教師、リモートワーク用書斎、Zoom映えメイクなどである。このように「私たちは技術と結びつくことで以前とは異なる存在へと変化するのであり、その変化を前もって完全に理解することも予想することもできない」[9]のである。ここでの関係は、人間＋Zoom→リモートワークという一義的な関係ではなく、人間と非人間が結びつくことで多種多様な存在様態へと変容する媒介的な関係になることを示している。そして私たち自身も、純粋な「人間」という存在に還元することができない。私たちは日々、「冷蔵庫人間」「道路人間」「スマホ人間」として生きているのである。技術は人間の生の背景的設定にもなり、身体化されてサイボーグ的連合体にもなる。ラトゥールは「何事も他の何かに還元されることはなく、あらゆるものは他のものに結びつきうる」[10]と述べている。この「非還元の原理」は、自然や社会を安定した存在として見なすことをやめ、具体的な諸要素へと目を向けさせる。これは技術決定論でもなく、社会構築主義でもない、予測不可能なハイブリッドが生み出されるという生成としての存在論なのである。

こうした生成的な事物への理解のもとで、設計者はハイブリッドの望ましくない帰結を回避するようにデザインの方向性を示さなければならない[11]。そして既存の建設システムのなかで形成されている諸要素の結びつきを明らかにし、それらを分析したうえで個別の実践に適したネットワークへと組み替えることができる。こうした事物連関の繋ぎ直しが建築の生態学的転回の主要な方法となるだろう。

事物連関のなかで建築をデザインするには、建築には所与の自律も他律も存在しないと認めることから始めないといけない。建築が自律しているとは、建築が建築以外のいかなる要素からもその成立のための影響を受けていない状態であり、建築が建

築それ自体に内在する原理によって成立している建築である[12]。その逆は他律的建築と呼ばれる。こうした自律と他律の対比的原理から、建築は完全な自律でもなく他律でもなく、その中庸の状態に存在すると想定することが可能になる。これは、建築はコンテクストから無関係でよいとする「強い自律」[13]と比較すると「弱い自律」と呼んでいいだろう。こうした創作の態度は、建築そのものの形を「自律」に還元し、さらに建築以外の要素を「他律」に還元したうえで、両者を折衷した方法論になっている。弱い自律を創作論に用いた途端に、建築の形式は創作者の任意で設定可能なものとしたうえで、敷地、施主の要望、予算、敷地、環境などの諸条件によって建築の形式が変形するという方法で統合される。この方法によって建築が場所性や歴史性などのコンテクストに配慮しているという言説を簡単に産出する仕組みになってしまっている。弱い自律の考え方を下敷きにすると、事物は建築との対応物に成り下がり、建築の形も無根拠なまま放置されてしまう。

事物連関のなかで存在するのは諸要素の集積のみである。こうした認識において建築の創作は、事物の成り立ちを追跡し、それらを組み替え、繋ぎ直すことになる。建築家は「Form Giver」（形を与える者）という役割に先んじて「Things Follower」（事物を追う者）なのである。建築の形は事物連関の中から湧き上がり、事後的に結晶化されるべきである。それはすでに確定された「原型」の建築ではなく、ありあわせのものをその都度集めた「雑種」の建築である。ただし、それはただの集積ではなく、物質やエネルギーの摂理に沿った精緻なデザインであるべきである。

本書では、都市や生態系における建築を取り巻く事物連関と設計行為に焦点を当てる。純粋無垢な原生自然ではなく、都市の生態系のなかの建築は利用可能な資源を寄せ集めたハイブリッドとなることを示し、事物を追跡することで得られるさまざまな物質への理解や解釈が、建築の構成法を発想する起点となることを示す。特に循環の基盤となる土壌と、生命のエネルギーの源

である太陽に着目する。現代人はインフラを通じて電気・ガス・水が利用できるため、太陽や土壌の力を軽んじている。しかし太陽なしには地球は熱力学的な意味において安定することはできないし、土壌なしには腐敗や分解が生じないのである。現代においてもなお、私たちは太陽と土の間にいる存在なのである。

註

1――映画『フード・インク』(2008)。ロバート・ケナー監督・脚本によるアメリカの食品産業の問題に切り込んだドキュメンタリー映画。

2――「人新世（Anthoropocene）」とは気候学者パウル・クルッツェンが提唱した新たな地質学的時代区分の呼称で、人類の活動が地球の生態系と大気に決定的な影響を及ぼすようになった時代のことである。クリストフ・ボヌイユ＋ジャン゠バティスト・フレソズの『人新世とは何か――〈地球と人類の時代〉の思想史』(野坂しおり訳、青土社、2018／原著＝2013) では、過去2世紀半の間、絶え間なく存在してきた環境にまつわる知識と警告を無視して歩み続け、工業化・消費主義的活動に反対するオルタナティブな選択を圧殺してきたとし、金融化した資本主義を新たな「脱抑制」の形式であると批判している。

3――鬼頭秀一『自然保護を問い直す――環境倫理とネットワーク』(ちくま新書、1996) において、1970年代における環境倫理思想は、自然保護から環境主義へと向かい、人間中心主義の脱却が目指され、当時の思想の特徴は動物解放論、自然物の当事者適格の概念、ディープエコロジーの3つの考え方とされる。これに対し、ティモシー・モートン『自然なきエコロジー――来たるべき環境哲学に向けて』(篠原雅武訳、以文社、2018／原著＝2007) では、ディープエコロジーを念頭に、有機体が生み出す崇高なホーリズムとしての自然観を批判し、純粋無垢な自然は想定できないとした。また気候変動が深刻化する現在において、例えば篠原雅武『人新世の哲学――思弁的実在論以後の「人間の条件」』(人文書院、2018) では、地球は私たちが住むための場所として存在していないという惑星そのものの他性という認識において、人間世界の根底を再設定することが求められていると述べられている。

4――ウィリアム・マグダナー＋マイケル・ブラウンガート『サステイナブルなものづくり――ゆりかごからゆりかごへ』(岡山慶子＋吉村英子監修、山本聡＋山崎正人訳、人間と歴史社、2009／原著＝2002) では、公共の利益のために規制が必要であるが、規制が「加害のライセンス」になり、政府が企業に与える「許容できる」速度と割合で病気や破壊をもたらしてもよいという許可証になる危険性を指摘している。また効率そのものに価値はなく、効率自体は、より大きなシステムの一部にしかすぎず、効率の是非はシステムが生み出す価値によって決まり、システムそのものの目的がいかがわしいものであるときには効率は意味をなさないと指摘している。

5――難波和彦『新・住宅論』(法政大学叢書、2020)「エコハウスというテーマはPCなのである。デザインの特異性を追求する建築家にとって、あまりにも正しいテーマは建築家としての売り物になりにくい」181頁

6――ピーター゠ポール・フェルベーク『技術の道徳化――事物の道徳性を理解し設計する』(鈴木俊洋訳、法政大学出版局、2015／原著＝2011) 155頁

7――「サイエンスウォーズ」と呼ばれる科学者と科学論者の論争。科学知識の

社会学による科学の相対主義的理解が科学者の反発をもたらし、生物学者グロスと数学者レヴィットによる『高次の迷信』(1994)、物理学者アラン・ソーカルによる擬似論文が掲載された「ソーカル事件」、ソーカルとジャン・ブリクモンによる『知の欺瞞——ポストモダン思想における科学の濫用』(田崎晴明＋大野克嗣＋堀茂樹訳、岩波現代文庫、2012／原著＝1997)のポストモダン言説批判などへと発展した。

8——ブルーノ・ラトゥール、ミッシェル・カロン、ジョン・ローによる社会科学の理論。「自然」も「社会」も前提にせず、行為性をもたらす連関をアクターに従って丹念に辿ることによりさまざまな事象が分析される。アクターネットワーク論においては「アクター」と「ネットワーク」は分離されず、アクターの働きによって異種混交のネットワークが生み出され、アクターはネットワークの働きによって定義され、変化を被る。

9——久保明教『ブルーノ・ラトゥールの取説』(月曜社、2019) 69-70頁

10——同書、55頁

11——ピーター＝ポール・フェルベーク『技術の道徳化——事物の道徳性を理解し設計する』(鈴木俊洋訳、法政大学出版局、2015／原著＝2011) 170頁

12——坂牛卓『建築の設計力』(彰国社、2020) 29頁

13——篠原一男「住宅設計の主体性」(『住宅論』鹿島出版会、1970、158-177頁) を参照。建築家の篠原一男は、住宅は、都市・敷地・予算・施主から自由でなければならないとした。

Refined Mongrels:

Tracing the Relationship between Things, and Rearranging and Reconnecting Them

In the meat aisle of the supermarket, I was seized by a strange sensation. I suddenly recalled a sequence from a documentary film.[1] In it an enormous number of chickens were herded into a dark, cramped shelter and injected with vaccines to prevent infections. Overfed chickens too fat to support their own weight stood up only to sit down again. The carcasses of slaughtered chickens were divided up into pieces (thighs, breasts, white meat, etc.), covered with plastic wrap, and lined up in neat rows. In the supermarket where I now stood, however, all signs that animals and plants are living things had been removed, and the shelves were instead stocked with signifiers of foods. In an artificial environment, clean and well-maintained for human beings, it feels like humans are the world's only inhabitants.

We inhabit a world in which human-generated systems have grown too vast. The cumulative effect of all this human activity has come to exert a global impact, causing deviations in the Earth's stable climate, and we are entering the overheated and contaminated geological epoch known as the Anthropocene.[2] Phenomena exceeding the scale of human power, such as the Great East Japan Earthquake and the subsequent accident at the Fukushima No. 1 Nuclear Plant, typhoons and torrential rains caused by climate change and pandemics, demonstrate that the artificial environment we have created is spiraling out of control.[3] We must construct spaces to inhabit even under these fragile and volatile conditions.

The increase in greenhouse gases such as carbon dioxide, caused by the use of fossil fuels like oil and coal, is believed to be a major source of global warming and other climatic changes. This has unquestionably led to an urgent need for a reduction in energy consumption and carbon dioxide emissions in the construction and utilization of buildings. However, it is important to consider the notion of sustainable development. How much thought has the construction industry put into building in a sustainable manner? I do not mean to cast any doubt on the building process itself, nor am I criticizing efforts to save energy and reduce carbon dioxide. But these methods have merely been implemented in areas that have already been identified as the cause of a problem. This runs the risk of justifying existing systems.[4] In architecture that is conceived as subordinate to efficiency, only measurable numbers have value, and individual sensual experiences and creative strength has a tendency to be neglected or completely ignored.[5] Ecology is a system of interactions between living things and the environment, encompassing myriad life activities of production, consumption, and decomposition, and it involves addressing fundamental questions about how diverse living and human-made objects coexist. Because the elements that make up ecosystems and the relationships among them are so complex, maximizing efficiency is not an across-the-board solution, and we need the flexible and receptive ecological sensitivity to accept various kinds of relationships with non-human beings and ecological ways of living that emerge from these interactions. What I want to present is not a utopian vision for the future in which problems are solved by innovation in science and technology, nor is it an architectural aesthetic in which beauty transcends real-world problems. It is a vision of generative architecture, far removed from sterile-sounding "sustainability," which emerges when we find ways to get along somehow amid decomposition and decay.

Architecture is a kind of technology. It is both a construction technology, and a living technology. The artificial entities made by a designer play an intermediary role in human actions and experiences.[6] While they do not unequivocally determine the quality of life, they do to a certain extent intervene in how our lives are shaped. There are two contrasting positions regarding science and technology and society: technological determinism, which holds that society is defined by science and technology, argues that scientific knowledge and technologies exist independently of society, while social constructivism sees scientific and technological pursuits as social activities and stresses that society is made up of many different types of knowledge. Amid the bitter debate between these two models,[7] Bruno Latour's actor-network theory[8] questioned whether it was even possible to reduce science and technology to either nature or society. In actor-network theory, various phenomena are analyzed by carefully tracing relationships among things and phenomena in terms of "actors," which are not limited to human beings alone. Non-human entities, and those that have changed into other entities are also considered to be actors. Humans and non-humans are not mutually independent, and because they are connected in a network made up of a mixture of many different things, their existential state is subject to change. For example, the number of people using the Zoom video conferencing system increased due to the spread of the coronavirus. This link between two different entities, Zoom and humans, triggered the emergence of a new hybrid called "Zoom humans." This term refers to office workers who are teleworking while doing the housework and taking care of their children; musicians who perform on online; participants in Zoom drinking parties; people establishing remote-work rooms in their homes, and those doing their makeup so that it looks good on Zoom. In other words, "Through our connection with technology, we are changing into a different entity than we were in the past, and we cannot expect to completely understand these changes at this earlier stage."[9] This is not a unilateral relationship such as "Humans + Zoom = remote work." Instead, creating a link between human and non-human entities suggests an intermediary relationship in which things are transformed into various states of existence. Thus, many types of technology are also a product of the interactive relationship between humans and non-humans. Moreover, it is no longer possible for us return to a purely human existence. We live our daily lives as "refrigerator humans," "road humans," and "smartphone humans." Latour talks about "how nothing can reduced to anything else, and how all things are linked to something else."[10] This non-reductionist principle calls attention to a wide range of concrete factors while avoiding the assumption that nature and society are stable entities. This is an ontology as generation of an unpredictable hybrid that is neither technical determinism nor social constructivism.

Designers must present design directions that enable avoidance of undesirable consequences related to hybrids, based on an understanding of these generative phenomena.[11] And by clarifying the links between various factors that are shaped by existing construction systems, they can analyze and rearrange them into a network that is adequate for individual use. Reconnecting the relationships between things is a primary means of achieving an ecological turning point in architecture.

To design structures in the context of relationships among things and phenomena, architecture must start with the recognition that there is no given autonomy or heteronomy. Architectural autonomy hinges on a situation in which architecture is realized independent of all non-architectural elements and their influence. This means that architecture is generated according to the principle that architecture is inherent to itself.[12] The opposite of this might be termed "heteronomous architecture." Based on these contrasting principles of autonomous and heteronomous, we can assume that architecture is neither one thing nor the other, but rather that it exists in an intermediate state. This can be called "weak autonomy," as opposed to "strong autonomy,"[13] which states that architecture stands independent of context. The latter reduces the form of the architecture to an autonomy, and by further reducing the extraneous elements to a heteronomy, gives rise to a methodology in which the two are blended. This methodology of "weak autonomy" leads to a system in which architectural style is arbitrarily configured by the designer, and then integrated in such a way that the form of the building changes depending on various conditions such as the site, the owner's requests, the budget, and the environment. This method leads to a system that easily produces descriptive language with a contextual awareness of things such as locality and history. With an approach based on weak autonomy, things and phenomena become mere counterparts of architecture, and the forms of architecture are left without any foundation.

In relationships among things, the only thing that exists is an accumulation of various elements. Based on this recognition, the creation of architecture becomes a process of tracing things, and rearranging and reconnecting them. Before taking on the role of "giver of forms," the architect should first function as a "follower of things." Architectural forms should emerge from the relationship between things and crystalize after the fact. This is not an architecture of established models, but a "mongrel" architecture made up of a collection of things that happen to be available in each particular instance. However, such architecture should be not simply a process of accumulation, but one of refined design aligned with the gifts that matter and energy present.

This book focuses on relationships and design practices surrounding architecture in cities and ecosystems. It makes the case that architecture in urban ecosystems, rather than a pure, pristine and innocent natural environments, is a hybrid of available resources, and that understanding and interpretation of the various materials obtainable by tracing the paths of things and phenomena constitute the starting point for imagining methods of architectural design. In particular, this book focuses on soil, the basis of life cycles, and the sun, the source of energy for life. Because of infrastructure that enables us to utilize electricity, gas, and water, contemporary people disregard the power of the sun and soil. However, without the sun the Earth could not be thermodynamically stable, and without soil, nothing would biodegrade or decompose. Even today, we are life forms inhabiting the zone between sun and soil.

Notes

1——*Food, Inc.* (2008) is documentary film directed and written by Robert Kenner which delves into the problems of the American food industry.

2——The term "Anthropocene" was popularized by the atmospheric chemist Paul Crutzen to refer to a new geological era, one in which human activities exert a decisive influence on the earth's ecosystem and atmosphere. In Christophe Bonneuil and Jean-Baptiste Fressoz's *The Shock of the Anthropocene: The Earth, History and Us* (2013; English edition, Verso, 2016), the authors criticize monetized capitalism as a new form of disinhibition for suppressing alternative forms of industrial and commercial activities, and for constantly ignoring information and warnings related to the environment for 250 years.

3——In his book *Reconsidering Nature Conservation: Environmental Ethics and Networks* (Chikuma Shinsho, 1996), Shuichi Kitoh discusses how in the 1970s advocates of environmental ethics shifted from nature conservation to environmentalism with an eye to extricating themselves from anthropocentrism. At the time, the philosophy was distinguished by three key concepts: animal emancipation, the moral standing of natural objects, and deep ecology. Meanwhile, in his book *Ecology Without Nature: Rethinking Environmental Aesthetics* (Harvard University Press, 2007), Timothy Morton criticized this view of nature as an organically derived form of sublime holism, based on deep ecology, and argued that nature could not be seen as pure and immaculate. In his book *Philosophy in the Anthropocene: The Human Condition in the Wake of Speculative Realism* (Jimbun Shoin, 2018), Masatake Shinohara discusses the perception of the Earth as a planet that does not exist solely as a place for us to live, and expresses the need to reestablish the foundations of human society as climate change grows increasingly severe.

4——In Michael Braungart and William McDonough's *Cradle to Cradle: Remaking the Way We Make Things* (North Point Press, 2002), the authors point out that despite the need for regulations that are in the public's interest, these measures can in some cases be a "license to harm" – a permit issued to a corporation by the government to dispense sickness and death at an "acceptable" rate and speed. Moreover, efficiency has no value – it is nothing more than one part of a larger system. The pros and cons of efficiency are determined by the value produced by the system, and because the objectives of that system are questionable at best, at some point, efficiency comes to be meaningless.

5——Kazuhiko Namba, *New Housing Theory* (Hosei University Press, 2020), p.181: "An 'eco-house' is a politically correct theme. To an architect who is striving for an idiosyncratic design, the theme is too correct to be marketable."

6——Peter-Paul Verbeek, *Moralizing Technology: Understanding and Designing the Morality of Things* (University of Chicago Press, 2011). p.155.

7——The so-called "science wars" were a series of intellectual exchanges between scientists and scientific realists. The relativist understanding of science favored by the sociology of scientific knowledge caused a backlash among scientists, prompting criticisms of postmodern discourse. These critical views include the biologist Paul R. Gross and the mathematician Norman Levitt's *Higher Superstition* (The Johns Hopkins University Press, 1994); the so-called "Sokal Affair" in which the physicist Alan Sokal published a paper that was actually a hoax; and Sokal and Jean Bricmont's book *Fashionable Nonsense: Postmodern Intellectuals' Abuse of Science* (first published in French, Editions Odile Jacob, 1997).

8——This sociological theory was developed by Bruno Latour, Michel Callon, and John Law. Avoiding the premise of nature or society, the writers analyzed a variety of phenomena by carefully tracing the relationships between actors that culminated in sexual acts. According to the actor-network theory, a mixture of different networks are generated through the activities of an actor, who is inseperable from the network, enabling the actor to define and undergo change based on the network's function.

9——Akinori Kubo, *A Guide to Bruno Latour* (Getusyosha, 2019), pp.69-70.

10——*Ibid.*, p.55.

11——Peter-Paul Verbeek, *Moralizing Technology: Understanding and Designing the Morality of Things* (University of Chicago Press, 2011). p.170.

12——Taku Sakaushi, *The Design Power of Architecture* (Shokokusha, 2020), p.29.

13——I referred here to Kazuo Shinohara's "The Independence of Residential Design" (*Essays on Residential Housing*, Kajima Institute Publishing, 1970, pp.158-177). As an architect, Shinohara held that residential architecture must be free from the constraints of city, site, budget, and owner.

賞味期限切れ都市と
新品都市

　第二次世界大戦後、多くの国々で人口の増加、都市化、工業化、農業の大規模化が起こった。大加速（Great Acceleration）と呼ばれる時代である。この時期から二酸化炭素の排出量の増加、オゾン層の破壊、地球温暖化、環境汚染、生態系の破壊などが急激に進行した。経済成長とともに、大量生産・大量消費・大量廃棄を前提とした産業構造に依存した生活様式が組み立てられていった。すでに人間の活動は地球のバイオキャパシティを超えている。

西大井周辺の上空からの風景。東海道新幹線とJR横須賀線が上下に重なっている
An aerial view of the Nishioi area. The Tokaido Shinkansen and JR Yokosuka Line tracks are layered one atop the other

　東京という大都市も大加速時代の産物である。それが今、朽ち始めている。日本の人口は2014年を境に減少に転じ、各地で空き家や空き店舗が増加している。これまでのスクラップ・アンド・ビルドの方法ではなく、既存ストックを活用することが求められている。しかしながら東京の都市中心部において建物は経済成長の道具になっている。オフィスビル、タワーマンショ

ン、商業施設は、再開発事業によってつねに新品でクリーンな状態にアップデートされている。他方、都市周縁部は戸建住宅と小規模アパートが集合する人々の居住地域だ。人口減少と超高齢化によって、この地域は疲弊して朽ちていくように見える。東京には新品都市と賞味期限切れ都市が並存しているようだ。賞味期限切れの都市では、インフラやサービスが新しく取り替えられないままに生活は続いていく。そこでは廃棄物が資源として読み替えられ、小さな更新が行われる。それは例えば空き家の縁側から、古いショップフロントから、放置された庭から、使われなくなったオフィスから始まっている。まるで賞味期限切れの食べ物を糧に菌類が成長するように。

　都市における暮らしは建物だけで完結しない。網目のように張り巡らされた生態系のなかで成り立っている。生きるためには、エネルギー、水、食べ物、材料などが必要で、これらは都市インフラから届けられている。建物はこうしたインフラに依存している。しかし太陽・土・大気などの自然の資源にアクセスすることで、都市のインフラに依存しすぎず、建物が自律性を獲得することができるはずだ。太陽の力によって暖房や給湯、さらには電力をつくることができる。土のなかにいる微生物の力で生ゴミや排泄物を分解することができる。クールスポットからの大気の流れを引き込めば、涼を得ることができる。また都市のなかでは大量に廃棄物が発生している。工事現場で余った材料や解体されて捨てられる建材を資源として再利用することができる。このように都市のなかにあるエネルギーと物質の循環を建物に引き込むことができるのだ。

　私たちの建築実践は、資源を見出すところから始まる。新品からではなくゴミと考えられるものから始まる。そしてお金をかけずに、太陽・土・水・大気といった自然資源を建物のなかに取り入れることを始めている。それが現代都市に居住するリアリティなのだ。

The Expired City and the Brand-New City

After World War II many countries experienced population growth, urbanization, industrialization, and a shift from family farms to large-scale agribusiness. It was known as the era of the Great Acceleration. This period also saw massive increases in carbon dioxide emissions, and rapid worsening of ozone layer depletion, global warming, environmental pollution, and ecosystem destruction. Along with economic growth came the advent of lifestyles dependent on the industrial structure, which was premised on mass production, mass consumption, and mass disposal. Today, human activity has already exceeded the Earth's biocapacity.

The megacity of Tokyo is also a product of the Great Acceleration, but it is now falling into decline. Japan's population peaked and began shrinking in 2014, and the number of vacant houses and stores is increasing nationwide. This situation calls for utilizing existing stock instead of the scrap-and-build approach prevalent thus far. However, in the Tokyo city center new construction is an engine of economic growth, and with ongoing redevelopment projects, gleaming new office buildings, high-rise apartment towers, and commercial facilities are constantly rising in place of their predecessors. Meanwhile, in largely residential peripheral areas of the city, where people live in detached houses and small apartment buildings, the declining and superannuated population is leading to a cityscape that appears exhausted and decaying. It seems that two cities coexist in Tokyo, one fresh out of the box, the other past its expiration date.

In urban areas past their expiration date, life goes on without new improvements to infrastructure and services. Discarded materials are seen as resources, and minor impromptu updates are made here and there. This can be seen on the ground-level verandas of unoccupied houses, in aged storefronts, in abandoned gardens, in disused offices. The process is like using expired food as fertilizer to grow fungi.

There is more to urban life than buildings. Life takes place within an ecosystem stretched like a web across the city, and requires an urban infrastructure supplying necessities such as energy, water, food and other goods. Buildings are dependent on this infrastructure, but they ought to be able to mitigate this dependence and increase their autonomy by accessing natural resources such as sunlight, soil and air. Solar power can be used for heating, hot water, and to generate electricity. Microorganisms in the soil have the power to decompose kitchen garbage and even human waste. Cooling can be achieved by drawing in air flow from cool spots, i.e. places where cooler air tends to accumulate. Also, large quantities of waste materials are generated in the city. Surplus materials from construction sites, and building materials dismantled and discarded when buildings are demolished, can be reused as resources. In this way, buildings can draw on the city's energy and material cycles.

Our architectural practice begins with the discovery of resources, not with brand-new products but with things dismissed as trash. And we are beginning to incorporate natural resources such as sun, soil, water, and air into buildings. By doing so, we engage with the realities of life in the present-day city.

《西大井のあな》外観と坂道
Holes in the House (Casa a Nishioi)
exterior and inclined street

左：《西大井のあな》の穴の見上げ
右：《西大井のあな》3階の階段
Left: Looking up through the holes in *Holes in the House (Casa a Nishioi)*
Right: *Holes in the House (Casa a Nishioi)* third-floor staircase

都市のワイルドエコロジー

《西大井のあな》のサブタイトルに「都市のワイルド・エコロジー」と名づけた。都市とワイルド（野生）は矛盾した言葉だ。私たちがこの言葉に投影したのは、都市のなかに自生する雑草のような強さだ。アスファルトやコンクリートの人工物のわずかな隙間で生きるしぶとさである。都市にはすでに建物がたくさんある。だったらこの構築物を切り拓いて自らの住まいをつくろう。

　住まいを探すなかで私たちが選んだ場所は、品川や東京、渋谷や新宿へ乗り換えなしでアクセスできる西大井である。戦前、戦中にかけて光学機器などの軍需工場が立地しており、そこで働く労働者が住んでいた。低地と台地が入り組んだ地形のため、大規模な宅地開発の手が入らず、西大井は品川区で最も地価の安いエリアである。路地には密集する木造住宅、道路沿いにはマンションがあり、所々にさびれて閉まったままの商店、朽ちた空き家がある。衰微していく都市の予兆が感じられる。経済が停滞し、もはや新しく建てることさえ難しくなっている現実のなかで何ができるのか。

　私たちは西大井にあるバブル期に建てられた鉄骨4階建ての中古住宅と土地を購入した。予算が限られていたため、解体直後に引越し、住みながら自分たちで少しずつ改修し始めた。しかしこんな雑草のような些細な計画であっても、実際に土地と家屋の購入を進めていくと、住宅産業、不動産業、金融業、保険業、各種制度が強く連携してシステムが整備されていることがわかった。自分の命と引き換えに借金をするのである。それが当たり前のルールのように説明される。そして深く考えさせないように道筋が引かれている。そこから脱線すると家なんてつくれない。「家について考える必要はありませんよ、家はすでに用意されていますから」と社会が囁いているようだった。家はもはや成長時代に整備された効率的で経済優先の産物だった。家を自由に考えてつくる権利が奪われているのか。

　「ワイルド」とはこうした硬直した思考停止状態から抜け出

す言葉だ。都市にある構築物（この場合は安価な中古住宅）を壊す。壊したところに「あな」が出現する。これは床スラブに開いた物理的な「あな」であると同時に社会制度に対する空隙としての「あな」である。この壊された状態＝「あな」から新しい野生が発生する。野生とは生きる力、考える力、つくる力だ。

　都市のなかでの暮らしは建物だけで完結しない。網目のように張り巡らされた生態系のなかで成り立っている。生きるためには、エネルギー、水、食べ物、資材などの資源が必要で、これらは通常、都市インフラから届けられる。建物はこうしたインフラに依存している。経済が停滞する社会で、はたして老朽

《西大井のあな》の模型（S=1/10）
1/10 scale model of *Holes in the House*
(*Casa A Nishioi*)

化が進むインフラにずっと頼れるのか。将来、建物は自律的な物質・エネルギー循環のシステムを持つ可能性が十分にある。しかもそれは最先端の技術やハイスペックなものでなく、どんな建物でも都市のなかの資源に安価にアクセスできるものであるはずだ。いやそうならないといけない。そのヒントとなるものを掴みたい。都市のなかでも簡単に得ることができる自然の資源は太陽のエネルギーである。暖房や給湯さらには電力をつくるのに太陽を利用しよう。また都市のなかでは大量に廃棄物が発生している。例えば工事現場で余った材料や解体されて捨てられる建材である。捨てられたゴミを資源として再利用しよう。都市のなかにあるエネルギーと物質の循環を建物に引き込もう。

　私たちはまず、積層するスラブの階段に隣接した1スパンに「あな」を開けた。狭い各階に立体的な広がりを効果的に得るため、階段を味方につけた。各階で異なる生活の場面を縦断するダイナミックな体験を日常に織り交ぜる狙いだ。既存の天窓や階段の窓から「あな」を介して薄暗かった2階のエントランスまで光が届けられる。次に倉庫だった1階を事務所として使えるように、無断熱のALCの外壁やコンクリート基礎に断熱を付加した。さらに床や壁の仕上げには廃材となった檜や杉の縁甲板を再利用した。人間がゴミとみなしてしまえば、あらゆるものがゴミになってしまう。すぐに捨てないで資源とみなして使う「もったいない精神」である。周辺の町並みには、かつて商店や工場として使われていた様子が見られるが、今はシャッターで

《西大井のあな》の穴の見下げ
Looking down through the holes in *Holes in the House (Casa a Nishioi)*

《西大井のあな》4階の寝室
Holes in the House (Casa a Nishioi)
fourth-floor bedroom

閉ざされている。この職住一体の住宅型は地域のポテンシャルとなるはずである。その実践例を示すべく、街から仕事場が見え、路地と繋がる大開口を設けた。これはペアガラスの樹脂サッシとした。角にある鉄骨柱の根元が雨樋からの雨水の侵入で錆びてボロボロに朽ちていたため鉄筋コンクリートで根巻きし、その厚みを利用してベンチを設けた。雨樋のルートを少々変えて雨水タンクと繋げ、集めた雨を水やりや災害時に利用する。また厄介者である鉄骨の柱や梁を覆っているロックウールの飛散を防止するために霧吹きを使って塗り固めた（ロックウール吹付は耐火材として安価だが使わないほうがいい）。天井の解体後に露出した電気配線やダウンライトはロープでブレースに縛り付けて固定した。今後は、屋上に太陽熱を集めるパネルを設置する。太陽で暖められたお湯は循環ポンプで1階の貯湯槽に送られ、暖房や給湯に利用する。1階の窓は北側にあるため冬のダイレクトゲインは望めない。外気温の影響を受けやすいペリメーターにお湯を引き回し、蓄熱体となるレンガで囲って効率的に暖房する。この暖房により温められた空気は「あな」を介して上昇する。最上階に溜まった暖気は「あな」を貫通するダクトによって下の階に送風され、熱が上へ下へと通り抜けて循環する。3、4階の外壁に断熱を付加し、内窓を設けて熱が逃げないようにする。4階の日当たりの良い南側の一部には、電車の騒音に対して防音を兼ねた洗濯室を設ける。敷地の北側にある駐車スペースの土間コンクリートを削って土壌に戻して植栽を植え、夏に涼風を得るためにクールスポットをつくる。壊すことで生じた「あな」を起点にして、建物が都市のなかの生態系と再び繋ぎ直されるのだ。

HOLES IN THE HOUSE

ROOF PLAN

THIRD FLOOR PLAN

BEDROOM · CLOSET · LAUNDRY

SECOND FLOOR PLAN

KITCHEN · BATH · LIVING/DINING · JAPANESE ROOM 1 · JAPANESE ROOM 2 · ENTRANCE · BATH

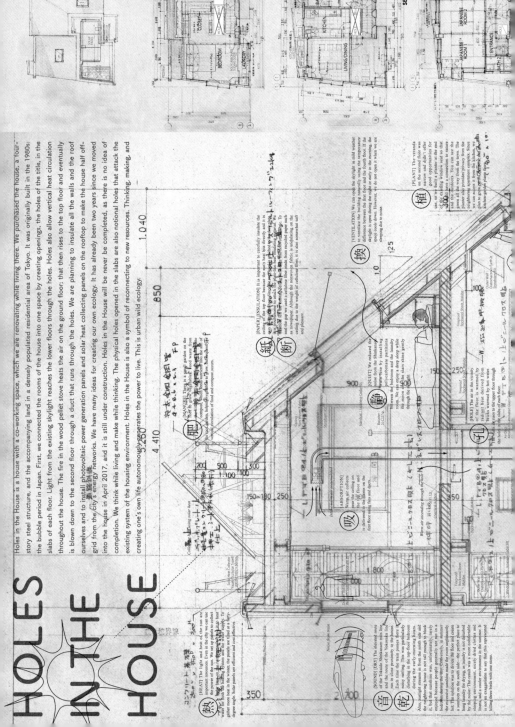

Holes in the House is a house with a co-working space, which we are renovating while living there. We purchased the house, a four-story steel structure, and the accompanying land in a densely populated residential area of Tokyo. It was originally built in the 1980s: the bubble period in Japan. First, we connected the rooms of the house into one space by creating openings: the holes of the title, in the slabs of each floor. Light from the existing skylight reaches the lower floors through the holes. Holes also allow vertical heat circulation throughout the house. The fire in the wood pellet stove heats the air on the ground floor; that then rises to the top floor and eventually is blown down to the second floor through a duct that runs through the holes. We are planning to insulate all the walls and the roof ourselves and to install photovoltaic power generation panels and solar heat collecting panels on the rooftop to make the house half off-grid from the city's energy networks. We have many ideas for creating our own ecology. Holes in the House will be never be completed, as there is no idea of into the house in April 2017, and it is still under construction. Holes in the House will be never be completed, as there is no idea of completion. We think while living and make while thinking. The physical holes opened in the slabs are also notional holes that attack the existing system of the housing environment. Holes in the House is also a symbol of reconnecting to new resources. Thinking, making, and creating one's own life autonomously generates the power to live. This is urban wild ecology.

1.040

850

.25

1.0

4.410

900

900

250

100

350

350

2.100

植 [PLANT] The veranda on the second floor was narrow and didn't offer good opportunities for use, so we built a planter at the end and grow plants there. If you make a connection to nature and the outdoors, you can see the greens all the way from the town. The planter also provides privacy from the neighboring house, and because we can access it from the kitchen, we plan to grow garden vegetables and herbs. Kitchen-garden planting through...

換 [VENTILATION] We can open the skylight in mild weather to ventilate the building naturally using the temperature difference between the fourth floor, where the skylight is open during the night or early in the morning, the space cools down. However, we do not open it when we are sleeping due to noise.

紙 断 [PAPER / INSULATION] It is important to carefully insulate the ceiling of the top floor because the sun's heat hits directly and it is... we used a cellulose fiber made from recycled paper such as newspaper. Although the nonwoven fabric is unsplitting on the ceiling due to the weight of cellulose fiber, it is also somewhat soft and pleasant.

肥 [MANURE] There is a small garden on the Roof to grow vegetables. Food waste from the kitchen is composted... To our garden, helping... circulation of food and compost occurs.

動 [QUIET] We reduced the noise from the Shinkansen train line by installing polyurethane partitions between the tracks... We can enjoy a deep sleep while this moon... the stairs shine gently through the night.

吸 [ABSORPTION] Warm air collects near the ceiling on the 3rd floor and is delivered to the first floor using fans and ducts.

排 [HOLE] The air in the vicinity of the floor is warmed by hung laundry for drying, as... the holes in the slabs of each floor... the air rises to the upper floor through the hole.

熱 [HEAT] The light and heat of the sun are important resources. Even in the city we can use the power of the sun. We set up panels to collect... gather more heat in the winter, the panels are tilted at a steep angle. Solar panels are efficient and cost effective.

宣 乾 [SOUND / DRY] The elevated route of the Tokaido Shinkansen runs like a wall, and the route of the Yokohama line is just beyond. Each time the train passes there is noisy rattling. This was particularly disturbing in the top-floor bedroom during the early-morning hours. Also, sunlight streaming in from the south was blocked by the neighboring house is not tall enough to block it, but that sunshine was, unfortunately, rarely exposed because people generally are out in a day and the excessive sunshine made the room unpleasantly hot. The solution was to divide the floor and create a sunroom on the south side—the perfect place to hang laundry for drying, as laundry is not disturbed by the morning train noise, and a cooler environment in the summer. It is not an exaggeration to say that this represented Killing three birds with one stone.

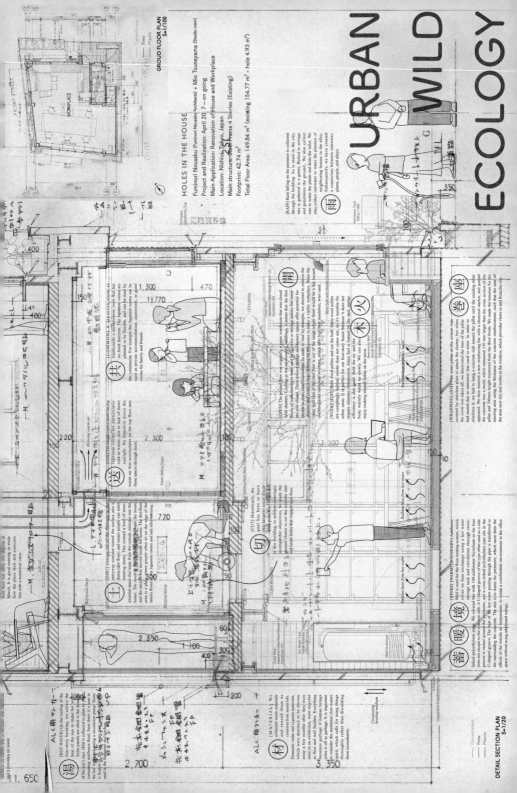

URBAN WILD ECOLOGY

HOLES IN THE HOUSE

Fuminori Nousaku (Fuminori Nousaku/architects) + Mio Tsuneyama (Studio mnm)
Project and Realization: April 20, 7 - on going
Main Application: Renovation of House and Workplace
Location: Nishicho, Tokyo, Japan
Main structure: Steel frame 4 Stories (Existing)
Footprint: 42.74 m²
Total Floor Area: 149.84 m² (existing 154.77 m² – hole 4.93 m²)

GROUD FLOOR PLAN S=1/100

DETAIL SECTION PLAN S=1/20

Urban Wild Ecology

Our project *Holes in the House (Casa A Nishioi)* is subtitled *Urban Wild Ecology*. "Urban" and "wild" sounds like a contradiction in terms, but for us the phrase implies the strength of weeds that grow naturally in the city. It implies the toughness that enables them to grow up through small cracks in the human-made asphalt and concrete. The city is already full of buildings, so we decided to take an existing structure and open it up to create a home of our own.

When looking for a house, the area we settled on was Nishioi, from which you can get to Shinagawa, Tokyo, Shibuya, and Shinjuku stations without changing trains. Munitions factories producing optical equipment and so forth were located here before and during World War II, and the neighborhood was home to workers at these plants. Large-scale residential development is not possible due to terrain with complex elevation differentials, and land values in Nishioi are the lowest in Shinagawa Ward. The district contains densely packed wood-frame houses along narrow lanes and apartment buildings along larger streets, and is dotted with run-down, shuttered stores and dilapidated vacant houses. One gets premonitions of the city's coming decline. What could we do with a previously owned house amid the realities of a stagnant economy, where even constructing a new one is a challenge?

We bought a pre-owned four-story, steel-frame house on a plot of land in Nishioi, which had been built during the economic bubble era (1986 – 1991). Having a limited budget, we moved in immediately after partially dismantling the structure, and gradually renovated the house ourselves while living in it. However, it turned out that even our modest little plan – analogous to a weed growing through a crack in the sidewalk – in practice involved the purchase of land and a house, and therefore was connected to the closely interlinked system of the housing, real estate, finance, insurance and other industries. In this system, people in effect put up their own lives as collateral to borrow money, and it is explained to them that this is simply the way of the world. Things proceed along well-oiled rails, so you do not need to think deeply. Go off these rails, however, and you will be unable to build anything. Society seems to be whispering, "There is no need to worry about a home, one is already prepared for you." There are plenty of homes built with priority on efficiency and economy, a legacy of the years of economic growth. Do we no longer have the right to think about the home we want to live in, and build it the way we want?

The word "wild" is key to breaking free of this rigid, mindless state. Our project was to take one of the city's existing structures (in this case an inexpensive pre-owned house) and partially dismantle it. Where the dismantled sections had been, there were now "holes." There were physical holes made by cutting through floor slabs, and at the same time holes in the sense of cracks in the social system, where something new and wild can grow in the space left after dismantling. In wildness is the power to live, think, and create.

《西大井のあな》
3階のリビング
*Holes in the House
(Casa a Nishioi)*
third-floor living room

There is more to urban life than buildings. Life takes place within an ecosystem stretched like a web across the city, and requires an urban infrastructure supplying necessities such as energy, water, food and other goods. Buildings are dependent on this infrastructure, but in a stagnated society, will we be able to rely on aging infrastructure indefinitely? It is quite possible that in the future, buildings will have autonomous systems for circulation of materials and energy. And these do not need to be state-of-the-art or top-of-the-line. Any building should – no, *must* – be able to have affordable access to resources available in cities, and we are exploring ideas for achieving this. One natural resource easily obtainable in the city is the sun's energy. Solar power can be used for heating, hot water,

《西大井のあな》1階の事務所
Holes in the House (Casa a Nishioi) first-floor office

and to generate electricity. Also, large quantities of waste materials are generated in urban environments. Surplus materials from construction sites, building materials dismantled and discarded when buildings are demolished, things disposed of as trash can be reused as resources. In this way, buildings can draw on the city's energy and material cycles.

We began by opening up "holes" in one span adjacent to the stairs, which consists of layered slabs. The idea was to make the stairway a partner in our effort to effectively broaden the spatial expanse of each claustrophobic floor of the house. We aimed to weave together a dynamic experience in which different scenes from daily life, on different floors, are interwoven. Through the "holes," light is introduced from the existing skylight and staircase windows to the dimly lit entrance on the second floor. Next, we added insulation to the uninsulated ALC outer wall and concrete foundation so that the first floor, which had been a warehouse, could be used as an office. To finish the floors and walls, we reused cypress and cedar strip flooring that had been scrapped. Anything can become trash if people regard it that way, but with a spirit of *mottainai* (a handy

Japanese word meaning "regret over something being wasted"), we can decide to turn something into a resource instead of discarding it immediately. In the neighborhood, many buildings once used as stores and small factories are now shuttered, and we believe that combined living and working spaces like this one have potential to revitalize the area. To show an example of this model in practice, we created a large aperture, in the form of double-glazed resin sash, that reveals the workspace to passersby and connects to the narrow lane in back. As the base of a steel column at the corner was rusted and falling apart due to rainwater leaking from the gutter, we wrapped it with reinforced concrete, making it thick enough to be used as a bench. We altered the route of the gutter slightly and connected it to a rainwater storage tank, and are using the collected rainwater to water plants and storing it in preparation for possible disasters. Also, we used spray damping to prevent troublesome rock wool covering the steel columns and beams from crumbling and scattering (sprayed-on rock wool is an inexpensive fireproofing material, but we advise against using it). After the ceiling was dismantled, electrical wiring and downlights were exposed, and these we fixed in place by tying them to braces with rope. In the future, we plan to install solar heat-collecting panels on the roof. Water heated by the sun will be transferred by a circulation pump to a storage tank on the first floor, and used for heating and hot water. The windows on the first floor face north, so in winter we cannot expect to gain heat directly from the sun. Hot water will be routed to the perimeter, which is easily affected by the outside air temperature, and enclosed by bricks serving to store heat, making for efficient heating. Air warmed by this heating will rise through the "holes," and warm air accumulated on the top floor blown down to the lower floors by a duct penetrating the "holes," so heat circulates both upward and downward. Insulation will be added to the outer walls on the third and fourth floors, and inner windows installed to hold in heat. A laundry room on the fourth floor, on the sunny south side, will be soundproofed against noise from passing trains. In the parking space on the north side of the site, concrete will be removed and the soil restored for planting, creating a cool spot generating breezes in the summer. We began by dismantling, creating holes in the structure. The outcome will be reconnection of the building to the urban ecosystem.

路地と家

新型コロナウイルス感染拡大によって、さまざまな距離が再考されつつある。他人との間には2mのフィジカルディスタンスの確保やマスクの着用が求められるが、家族の間ではフィジカルディスタンスは適応されず、家のなかでのマスク着用も推奨されたりはしない。この背景には家族はこれ以上分割できない共同体の単位であることが含意されている。家族が生活する器である住宅も問題だ。外出自粛により自宅で長時間過ごすことが増え、家族の距離は接近している。そのことでドメスティックバイオレンスが増えていると報道されている。住宅のなかに仕事部屋、学習部屋、書斎がなければ、リモート会議やオンライン授業に参加することが難しい場合もある。共働きの夫婦が同じ時間にZoom会議で互いの音声がストレスになることもあれば、小さな子どものケアをするために仕事ができないということもある。ワンルームマンションに住んでいる単身者は窒息しそうな狭小な空間に籠もらないといけない。このように外出自粛によって浮き彫りになったのは、私たちが生活している住宅は長時間過ごす居場所ではなく、一時的に時間を過ごす休息のための生存装置だという点である。新型コロナウイルスが蔓延する以前の日常では人々は多くの時間を家の外で過ごしており、家族はタイムシェアリングをしてうまくやり過ごしていたといえる。

現代の住宅の起源は近代の労働者住宅にある。近代社会では大量の人々が賃労働者として都市部に流入し、労働者は村落共同体に束縛されることなく、富を蓄積する主体として生活をするようになった。近代住宅はこうした労働者が疲れた体を休め、愛情で結ばれた夫婦が子どもを産み育てるための装置である。労働は住宅から分離され、工場や業務施設に集約された。労働者は朝起きて仕事に向かい、夜に帰宅してご飯を食べてテレビを見てお風呂に入って寝る。そうした生活プログラムが組み立てられた。さらに現代ではコンビニやスーパーマーケット、24時間営業の飲食店や各種サービスによって生活のアウトソーシ

路地の入り口に子供がチョークで書いた
「ここからぜったいにでないでね」
At the entrance of the lane a child wrote in
chalk: "DO NOT GO PAST THIS LINE"

ング化が進んでおり、多くの時間を住宅外で過ごすことが可能
になった。さまざまな生活行為のアウトソーシングのおかげで
家の狭小さに耐えることができてきたのである。これは経済成
長の道具として住宅建設を利用してきた住宅政策、新品主義で
次々に建て替える日本の習慣にも要因があるだろう。政府は外
出自粛によって家や家族が確固たる安定したシステムであるか
のように扱い、人々を家や家族の枠に閉じ込めようとする。し
かし、そもそも住宅のなかだけに人間の生活は閉じこもること
はできないはずである。

《西大井のあな》は一方は道路に、もう一方は袋小路の私道に
面している。この行き止まりになっている路地に面して13世
帯の家が建ち並んでいる。そのほとんどが50㎡程度の小さな土
地に建つ木造2階建の住宅である。新型コロナウイルスによる
外出自粛の時期には、この路地は子どもたちで活気に溢れてい
た。普段見かけないお父さんが子どもと一緒に遊んでいる。3
〜6歳ほどの子どもたちは三輪車で路地を駆け巡るのが好きな
ようで、通過交通のない路地は恰好の遊び場になった。ただし、
もう一方の車道は危険であるため、路地の入り口には「ここか
らはぜったいにでないでね」とアスファルトの黒い路面に白い
チョークで大きく書かれ、その境界を示す白いラインが描かれ

ていた。これは外出自粛という状況において、家という単位で閉じこもるのではなく、家々が集合する路地という単位で緩やかに繋がることを示唆していた。向かいの家には路地に面して洗濯物干し場のためのベランダがついているが、学校に行けない大学生が外の空気を感じながらキャンプ用の椅子に腰掛けて読書をしている。家のなかにずっといるのは息も詰まるのかもしれない。《西大井のあな》の庭はもともとコンクリートで塞がれていたためダンゴムシやミミズもいない死んだ土壌だったが、土を掘り起こして腐葉土と竹炭、生ゴミのコンポストを入れた。その後、微生物の菌糸が生え、雑草が生え、小さな虫が生息する、生命のいる庭になった。このような雑草や生ゴミ堆肥を受け入れた乱雑な庭は住宅地には珍しいようで、近所の方からマスク越しに話かけられることが増え、自生する雑草の名前や植物の世話の仕方を教えてもらったりする。

　こうした路地に現れた小さな気晴らしの風景から想像が膨らんでくる。住宅地の街区の内側に自動車は進入できないようにし、子どもが気兼ねなく遊べる袋小路があるべきだ。車が入らなければアスファルトで舗装する必要がないため地表面を土に戻すことができる。路地の入り口まで自動車や配達のトラックが寄り付くことができれば、そこに路地ごとにカーシェアのガレージと配達ポストがあればよく、路地の内側へのアクセス部分は歩行や車椅子のために少し舗装されていれば十分である。それぞれの家の屋根を流れる雨水をタンクに集めて路地の植栽の水やりに利用する。緑と土壌に覆われた路地に面して気晴らしのための半屋外のベランダや縁側があり、そこで路地で遊ぶ子どもを見守ったり、外を眺めて時間を過ごすことができる。この路地はほかの生命とともにいる気晴らしの居場所であり、共同の庭である。私たちは、近代都市が不潔であるとして排除してきた土を都市に取り戻し、家の居場所を外に押し拡げることができるはずである。そして閉ざされた家は都市に再び接続されるのである。

拙論「都市に再接続するための気晴らしの場所」（『現代思想』2020年8月号、青土社）を改編、加筆

Backstreet and Houses

The COVID-19 pandemic is causing us to reconsider distances in various ways. We are asked to maintain a physical distance of two meters from others and to wear masks, but physical distance recommendations do not apply among family members, and we are not told to wear masks at home. Underlying this is an implicit sense of the family as a basic community unit that cannot be subdivided. The residences that contain families are an issue as well. People are being encouraged to avoid going out as much as possible, they are spending more time at home, and family members are being drawn closer together, but it has been reported that this is leading to a rise in domestic violence. Without separate rooms for working and studying, it can be difficult to attend videoconferences and online classes at home. When both members of a couple are working, they may be stressed out by the sound of one another's voices when they have simultaneous Zoom meetings, or they may be unable to work because they must care for small children. Single people in studio apartments are confined to small spaces and may feel extremely claustrophobic. During this time of widespread self-quarantining, it has become clear that our homes have not been designed for continuous long-term occupancy, but as mechanisms for human survival that enable us to rest temporarily. Before the pandemic, people spent much of their time away from home, and one might say families maintained good relations through something like time-share arrangements.

The origins of contemporary dwellings lie in modern housing for laborers. With the Industrial Revolution there was a massive influx of people into urban areas, where they worked to earn wages, and workers come to be individual wealth-generating entities untethered from village communities. Modern housing developed as a mechanism for these workers to rest their tired bodies, and for couples – increasingly marrying for love rather than by arrangement – to have children and raise them. Labor was separated from residential space and concentrated in factories and other business-specific facilities. A behavioral program was established for mid-20th-century workers: get up in the morning, go to work, go home at night, eat, watch TV, take a bath, go to bed. In recent years, more and more of the procedures of daily life are outsourced to convenience stores, supermarkets, 24-hour restau-

《西大井のあな》の路地の土壌化
Converting the lane next to *Holes in the House (Casa a Nishioi)* into soil

rants and various other services, making it possible to spend much time outside the home. It is thanks to this outsourcing that we are able to endure living in very small spaces. Clearly a housing policy of utilizing residential construction as a tool for economic growth, and the Japanese practice of glorifying the new and rapidly demolishing and rebuilding, are key factors. When the government advises people to stay home, it assumes that homes and families are solid, stable systems, a framework in which to contain people. However, on a fundamental level our lives cannot be confined to our dwellings.

Holes in the House (Casa A Nishioi) faces the street on one side and a narrow, dead-end privately owned lane on the other. The latter is lined with residences, home to 13 households, most of them two-story wooden houses built on small plots of about 50 m2. When the stay-home advisory was in effect, the lane was a lively place overrun with romping children. Fathers we had never seen before were out playing with their kids. Children aged about three to six evidently enjoy riding tricycles up and down the lane, and being closed to through traffic, it makes a fine playground for them. However, the street on the other side is dangerous, and at the entrance of the lane it was written in large hiragana characters, in white chalk on black asphalt: "DO NOT GO PAST THIS LINE," with a white line indicating the boundary. This all suggests that under the circumstances of the stay-home advisory, instead of holing up separately as family units, households remained loosely connected, with the unit being the lane they all share. The house across from us has a balcony facing onto the lane intended for hanging laundry, but a university student kept home from school used it to sit in a camping chair and read while enjoying the outside air. Staying indoors all the time evidently felt suffocating. The garden of *Holes in the House (Casa A Nishioi)* originally contained dead soil with no pillbugs or earthworms, as it had been covered with concrete, but after the soil was turned over and humus, bamboo ash, and compost added, it became a living environment home to networks of microscopic mycelia, weeds, and small insects. Evidently a disorderly garden like this, where weeds are allowed to grow and compost is laid down, is rare in a residential area, and masked neighbors often talked to us, teaching us the names of wild-growing vegetation and how to care for plants.

The minor diversions one sees in a quiet lane like this spark the imagination. Residential areas ought to contain this kind of dead-end backstreet where cars cannot enter and children can play without fear. If there are no cars, there is no need to pave the street, and the ground can be converted from asphalt back into soil. If cars and delivery trucks can reach the lane's entrance, then it is sufficient to have car-sharing garages and postal delivery boxes for each lane, and light paving at the entrance to enable pedestrian and wheelchair accessibility. Rainwater dripping from the roofs of houses can be collected in tanks and used for watering plants in the lane. Facing the unpaved lane full of greenery could be semi-outdoor balconies and porches for recreation, where people can watch over their children playing or simply gaze at the outside world. A lane can be a place of diversion, where people engage with other lifeforms, as well as a communal garden. We have the potential to restore soil, which in modern cities has regarded as unsanitary and paved over, and expand our living spaces into the surrounding environment. This would reconnect each closed-off house to the city of which it is part.

Source: Fuminori Nousaku, "A Refreshing Place to Reconnect to the City," *Revue de la pensée d'Aujourd'hui*, August 2020, Seidosha, with revisions and additions

惑星規模のものと
身の回りのもの

　個別の建築と地球環境には大きなギャップがある。思想家ティ
モシー・モートン（1968-）は現代において「ハイパーオブジェ
クト」が人間の日常生活に多大な影響を与えていると述べてい
る。ハイパーオブジェクトとは何か。オブジェクトは身の回りに
ある「もの」であり、目に見えるから人間は知覚できる。それ
に対してハイパーオブジェクトはグローバルな規模のインパクト
を与えるが、はっきりと目に見えないし、人間の知覚を超えて
いるためにどのような挙動を示すか明確に予想できない。それ
は、例えば温室効果ガスであり、株価であり、放射性物質であ
り、ウイルスである。たしかに、地球環境問題のように惑星規
模の事象が私たちの日常生活に入り込んできている。CO_2をは
じめとする温室効果ガスによる温暖化は、気候変動や異常気象
を発生させ、日本では台風、酷暑、ゲリラ豪雨、洪水となって
猛威を奮っている。また、世界経済も惑星規模で影響を与えて
いる。例えばイギリスのEU離脱を巡る投票の結果は株価や物価
を変動させ、2008年の世界経済に影響を与えたリーマンショッ
クはアメリカのサブプライム住宅ローン危機によって引き起こさ
れた。中国武漢から発生した新型コロナウイルスは、感染症を拡
大させるだけではなく、中国のサプライチェーンを長期間に渡っ
て滞らせ、飛行機での国外移動をストップさせ、飲食店を閉鎖
させ、リモートワークを普及させた。これらの事象は、ある地
域に限定されて引き起こされるのではなく、惑星規模を伴って
引き起こされており、さまざまな要因が複合的に絡み合いなが
ら生じているため、人間の知覚を越えてしまっている。
　こうしたハイパーオブジェクトをなんとかコントロールし
ようとするために国際会議によって取り決めがなされ、国の政
策に反映される。COP（国連気候変動枠組条約締約国会議）や
G20（金融・世界経済に関する首脳会合）のような国際会議に
おいて各国の首脳級のトップがハイパーオブジェクトについて議

論し、解決策を模索し、惑星規模の問題が政策に沿って、法制度による規制、ガイドライン、補助金というかたちで私たちの日常生活にも入り込んでくる。惑星規模のハイパーオブジェクトに対して個別の建築はとても無力な存在なのだろうか。こうした状況のなかで個別の建築は、コスト、土地、前面道路、隣家、太陽、雨、風向き、庭、木材、鉄、コンクリート、ガラス、瓦、テレビ、ソファ、テーブル、ガスコンロ、洗濯機、ピアノ、衣類、家族、客、犬というような身の回りのものや人と、惑星規模で影響を与えるハイパーオブジェクトについて同時に気にしている。身の回りのものとハイパーオブジェクトには大きなギャップがあるが、同時に存在しているのだ。設計するということは、建築を介して現実の場所で小さな会議をしていることのように思える。個別の建築のなかで、身の回りのものと惑星規模のものが混交し、個々の場所の現実にぶつかりながら調停した結果として個々の建築がある。

　個別の場所や個別の条件が異なるからこそ、建築をボトムアップで組み立てていく可能性に開かれている。政策や産業がトップダウンでつくり出したものの連関に対して、現実との食い違いに気づき、場所に根ざした解決法を生み出すことができる。個別の場所での建築の組み立てが、惑星規模と身の回りのものに対して、どれが大事であり、どれがそこまで大事ではないのか、を決めていくことができる。そのことにより、建築は現実を批判し、それぞれの場所において居住するリアリティを構築することができる。建築はものの連関を見直し、産業や政策によって生み出された強固なものの連関を解きつつ、それらを再び縫合する存在になるべきだと思う。個別の場所には、家族がいて、太陽からの熱と光が届けられ、大気の流れがあり、雨が降り、緑が育ち、街並みがあり、風景がある。個別の場所にあるものや人は均質で無性格なのではなく、独特さに満ちている。建築は、ものや人の異なる種類の独特さを連関させて結び合わせていく。その結び合わせ方に現実とどう向き合ったかが自ずと現れてくる。

Planetary Scale and
Individual Human Scale

There is a great gulf between individual buildings and the global environment. The philosopher Timothy Morton (b. 1968) asserts that "hyperobjects" have an enormous influence on our daily lives in the current era. What is a hyperobject? While objects are the "things" around us that are visible and therefore perceptible, hyperobjects have a global impact but are not clearly visible, and as they are beyond human perception their behavior cannot be accurately predicted. Examples include greenhouse gases, the stock market, radioactive substances, and viruses. It is certainly true that planetary-scale events such as the global environmental crisis have become part of our everyday lives. Warming caused by greenhouse gases such as CO_2 is causing climate change and abnormal weather events, and typhoons, scorching heat, heavy localized downpours, and floods are rampant in Japan. The impact of economic events is also global in scope. For example, the outcome of the UK referendum on leaving the EU caused fluctuations in stock values and prices of goods, and the global financial meltdown of 2008 was triggered by the US subprime mortgage crisis. The novel coronavirus, which originated in Wuhan, China, not only causes COVID-19 but also halted China's supply chain for a long time, grounded overseas flights, forced restaurants out of business, and led to widespread adoption of remote work. Planetary-level events like this one do not occur only within limited areas, and they are caused by complex intertwining of various factors beyond the threshold of human perception.

International conferences are organized with the goal of controlling these hyperobjects, and their recommendations are reflected in national policies. At international conferences such as COP (Conference of the Parties, aka the UN Climate Change Conference) and the G20 (Group of Twenty, a forum for international economic cooperation), top-level officials from many nations discuss hyperobjects, explore solutions, and devise policies that affect our daily lives in the form of laws and regulations, guidelines, subsidies and so forth. Are individual works of architecture truly powerless in the face of planetary-scale hyperobjects? Under the current circumstances, designers of buildings are simultaneously concerned with things and people in our immediate surroundings – construction costs, land, roads in front of sites, neighboring houses, sunlight, rain, wind direction, gardens, lumber, iron, concrete, glass, roof tiles, TVs, sofas, tables, gas ranges, washing machines, pianos, clothing, family members, guests, dogs – and with hyperobjects that exert a global impact. There is indeed a large gulf between these human-scale objects around us and planetary-scale hyperobjects, but they coexist nonetheless. The design process appears to resemble a small group of people holding a face-to-face meeting on the topic of architecture. However, each individual piece of architecture is the outcome of intersections among human-scale things and global-scale systems, and of confrontation with the realities of the site and endeavors to mediate them.

When architecture are assembled from the bottom up, the possibilities are vast because each site is different and has its own unique conditions. While governmental policy and industry deliver top-down directives and guidelines, at the individual level it is possible to recognize discrepancies between these and realities on the ground, and to arrive at solutions rooted in specific sites. Architects can examine what is immediately at hand and what is occurring on a global scale, make decisions about which things are important and which are relatively unimportant in each particular case, and design architecture accordingly. This approach enables architecture both to critique reality and to construct the realities within which people reside at each site. I believe that architecture requires re-examining linkages among things, breaking ironclad connections forged by industry and policy when necessary, and stitching things back together. At each site there are real things and people – family members, the heat and light of the sun, the flow of air, rain, greenery, cityscape and scenery – and these are not faceless and homogeneous, but brimming with unique character. Architecture entails taking the unique features of all manner of things and people and causing them to relate and connect. Through this process, approaches to engaging with reality naturally emerge.

多敷地の感覚

建築を設計しているときに、実際に建物が建つ場所が唯一の敷地という感覚ではなくなっている。「一敷地」ではなく「多敷地」という考え方がしっくりくる。建築はさまざまな物質でできている。それらの物質を遡って追跡しようとすると、設計の対象は、建物がどのような材料でできていて、どこから調達されるかまで拡散していく。クライアントがたまたま所有している土地だけに建物を建てるのではなく、建物を建てるときに生じる影響は生産地や加工場やそこでの労働者にも及んでいる。物を追跡していくと、敷地はひとつではなく、さまざまな場所へと四方八方に広がっているように感じられてくるのである。

杉林の風景
A cedar grove

文化人類学や民族誌の用語でマルチサイテッド（Multi-sited）という言葉がある。従来の民族誌では、観察者はひとつのフィールドに長い時間を過ごし、そのフィールドに住まう人間の社会や文化について細かく記述する。しかしマルチサイテッド・エスノグラフィでは複数の現場で調査を行う。その理由のひとつは「物を追跡する」ことによって、事後的に調査の場所が増えていき、複数の現場になっていくことにあるのだそうだ。それがグローバル化した社会の民族誌のあり方なのかもしれない。

製材所の杉丸太
Stacks of cut cedar at a sawmill

この「多敷地」の感覚は、建築を設計する根拠も変容させる。例
えば建築には「一般解」と「個別解」という考え方がある。これ
は建築を問題解決の方法だと捉えた場合に想定される考え方で
ある。一般解はある敷地で成立する建築の考え方が、ほかの敷
地でも成り立つというアイデアである。どこに建ててもそのア
イデアが通用するというものである。例えば住宅不足の時代に
おいて量産型は、ほかの敷地でも通用し、大量に生産・反復で
きるため、価値がある考え方だろう。他方、個別解はひとつの
敷地、個別のクライアントだけにしか通用しない一度きりのアイ
デアである。もちろん個別解は特殊であるがゆえにユニークな
アイデアで満ちている。個別解はていねいに場所を読み解いた
り、クライアントの個性を汲み取ることができるだろう。

　こうした一般解と個別解の区別が存在することで、建築の
アイデアは普遍化する方向と具体化する方向の2つに切り裂か
れているように感じてしまう。そして往々にして一般解のほう

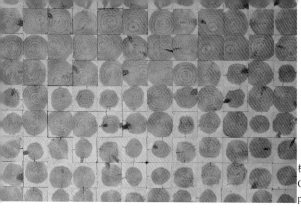

柱を再利用した杉のウッドタイル
Cedar tiles made from repurposed
pillars

が個別解より優れているとみなされることが多い。これはひと
つの敷地という考え方から生じているのではないか。どんな建
物も物質循環のなかに存在している。つまり多くの敷地にまた
がっていると考えるならば、一般解と個別解の区別は意味をな
さなくなり、どのような物質のネットワークのなかに建物は存
在しているのかという問いに書き換えられる。

　次に多敷地の考え方は、敷地の大きさに対する感覚も相対
化する。例えば、敷地が大きければ大きいほど大人数が使う公
共的な建築となり、私的で小さな建築よりも価値があるとされ
る。こうした考えも敷地がひとつしかないという感覚から生じ
るものである。たしかに建築の規模が大きいほどプロジェクト
に関わる人数も多く、時間もかかり、大事業である。しかしな
がら、多敷地の観点からすれば、建築の価値は、規模の大小で
はなく、物を追跡することによって事後的についてくる。

　このように多敷地の感覚は、一般解と個別解、規模の大小
によって建築の価値を確定しない。物を追跡することで、多く
の敷地に思考を巡らせ、実際に訪れ、人の話を聞き、素材に触
れることが大事になってくる。それは人類学の方法と似てくる
のではないか。建築家は諸々の事物を愚直に追跡する者になる
べきなのだ。

The Multi-Sited Mentality

Today, when one is designing architecture, the place where it will actually be built no longer seems to be the only "site." Here the concept of "multi-sited," as opposed to "single-sited," is a useful one. Buildings are constructed using a variety of materials, and when we endeavor to trace these materials back to their sources, the scope of design is diffused beyond the architecture per se to the materials it is made of and the sites at which these were procured. One does not simply building a discrete structure on land that the client happens to own – the impact of building it extends to the regions where materials are sourced, the plants where they are processed, and the workers at these sites. Tracking things in this way, one feels engaged with not just one site, but multiple sites expanding in all directions.

"Multi-sited" is a term used in cultural anthropology and ethnography. In traditional ethnography, field observers spent large amounts of time in one place and described the society and culture of people living there. However, in multi-sited ethnography, surveys are conducted at multiple sites. One reason is that through the process of "tracking things," the number of survey sites grows post facto and multiple sites come into play. Perhaps this is how ethnography must be approached in a globalized society.

氷見市中央商店街の防火建築帯
Himi City Central Shopping
Arcade firebreak zone

Adopting this "multi-sited" mentality also transforms the basis of architectural design. In architecture there are the concepts of "general solutions" and "specific solutions," premised on an interpretation of architecture as a means of solving problems. General solutions imply that architectural approaches that make sense as one site will make sense at other sites too, and ideas retain their validity no matter where structures are being built. For example, during housing shortages the general solution of mass-produced housing is valuable, as it can be applied at various sites and the mass production process can be repeated indefinitely. On the other hand, specific solutions are one-time ideas that only apply to single sites and individual clients. Of course, because they are unique, specific solutions are a rich source of original ideas. Specific solutions make it possible to decipher the peculiarities of a site thoroughly and design buildings that reflect clients' distinctive character.

This distinction between general and specific solutions makes it seem that architectural thinking can only go in one of two mutually exclusive directions: that of universalization, and that of case-by-case idea realization. General solutions are often considered superior to specific ones, but I believe this is a result of the single-sited mentality. In fact, every building is part of the larger material cycle. In other words, if we think of a building as spanning many sites, the distinction between general and specific solutions becomes meaningless, and the question is rewritten as: what is the nature of the material network to which the building belongs?

Also, a multi-sited mentality relativizes one's sense of a site's dimensions. A common premise is that the larger the site, the more likely the building is to be a public one used by numerous people, which is considered to have more value than a small, private build-

《考えるパンKOPPE》イートイン
スペース。120角材ひみ里山杉の
フレームと敷き詰められた
ウッドブロック
The eating area at *Kangaeru Pan Koppe (Thinking Bread Koppe)*. A frame of 120mm-square Himi Satoyama Sugi (Toyama cedar) timbers, and wood blocks laid flagstone-style

防火建築帯の一部にある《考えるパンKOPPE》
Kangaeru Pan Koppe (Thinking Bread Koppe), a bakery in the firebreak zone

ing. This premise also grows out of the single-sited mentality. To be sure, the larger the scale of a structure, the more people are involved in building it, the longer it takes, and the bigger the project becomes. However, from a multi-sited perspective the value of a structure is determined after the fact, not by its size but by tracking the things that went into making it.

Thus, with a multi-sited mentality one does not gauge the value of architecture depending on whether it represents a general or a specific solution, or by its scale. It becomes vital to consider a large number of sites, to visit them in person, to hear what people have to say, to engage with materials, in a manner similar to that of anthropologists. An architect must be someone who follows and frankly assesses all manner of things and phenomena.

背景への感触

2019年のヴェネチア・ビエンナーレ国際美術展の日本館展示「Cosmo-Eggs｜宇宙の卵」に参加した。美術家の下道基行、作曲家の安野太郎、人類学者の石倉敏明、建築家の能作文徳、キュレーターの服部浩之という異なる専門領域のメンバーが協働した。下道さんは津波石という大地震の際に津波の力で地上に押し流された岩石の映像、安野さんはゾンビ音楽と呼ばれるバルーンの空気圧でリコーダーを奏でる無人の機械演奏、石倉さんは沖縄や台湾などの神話を集めて創作した卵生神話を展示した。ふと自分に持ちネタ（移動可能な作品）というものがないことに気づいた。建築設計者はその都度の要望に応えているだけで、本当に自分がつくりたいものをつくってきたのだろうかと悩んでいた。プロジェクトの最初の段階で、日本館[1]を土に埋めたいと相談を受けたが、吉阪隆正[2]が設計した日本館をそのまま生かしたいと答えた。考えているうちにむしろ建築家である私の持ちネタは日本館そのものなのではないかと思うようになった。

　映像作品はリアプロジェクション（半透明フィルムに背面から投影）と呼ばれる方法で映し出される。スクリーンのサイズと投影距離が相関しているため、プロジェクターとスクリーンの結合した一体のフレームを設計し、映像が投影されている仕組み自体が現れるようにした。津波石の可動性に着目して、フレームにタイヤを付けてほかの場所にも移動できるようにし、日本館の卍型に配置された柱と柱の間に可動式スクリーンがおさまり、中央に向けてたまたま集まっているようにした。ゾンビ音楽にはリコーダーへ空気を吹き込むための巨大なバルーンと送風機が必要だ。送風機は風切音と振動音を発生させてしまう。日本館の展示室の床の中央には穴が空いており、ピロティと展示室が繋がっている。そこで送風機はピロティの下に、リコーダーは展示室に置かれ、バルーンは穴を貫通して塞ぎ、騒音が展示室に届かないようにした。日本館の壁面は真っ白に塗られて明るい室内になっていたが、映像を浮かび上がらせるために

薄暗い沼のような濁った緑色に塗装し、トップライトからの自然光とプロジェクションの光で照度を確保した。創作神話のテクストは壁に直接彫られ、その背後にある白いペンキと下地のMDFの質感がかすかに現れた。

　美術鑑賞の暗黙のルールに従えば、鑑賞者は、絵を見るときに、絵のフレーム自体や、展示室の空間そのものを除外して認識する。同じように、例えば本を読んでいると、紙やインクは背景に、文字情報は前景になる。このように人間はルールに沿って対象と環境を分離して認識しているようだ。しかし「Cosmo-Eggs｜宇宙の卵」では、展示室やフレームという背景が作品と渾然一体となって知覚に働きかける。無意識化された環境を少し前に押し出し、独特な知覚を生み出すことが建築家としての私の役割だった。背景がオブジェや彫刻のように対象化するのではなく、背景のままでありながら不思議な感触で迫ってくるのである。

註
1――ヴェネチア・ビエンナーレ日本館
　　　ジャルディーニ会場にあるパビリオン。吉阪隆正による設計、竣工は1956年。
2――吉阪隆正（1917‒80）
　　　日本を代表する建築家、ル・コルビュジエに師事、早稲田大学教授を務めた。

《Cosmo-Eggs》バルーンとスクリーン
Balloon and screen at *Cosmo-Eggs* exhibit

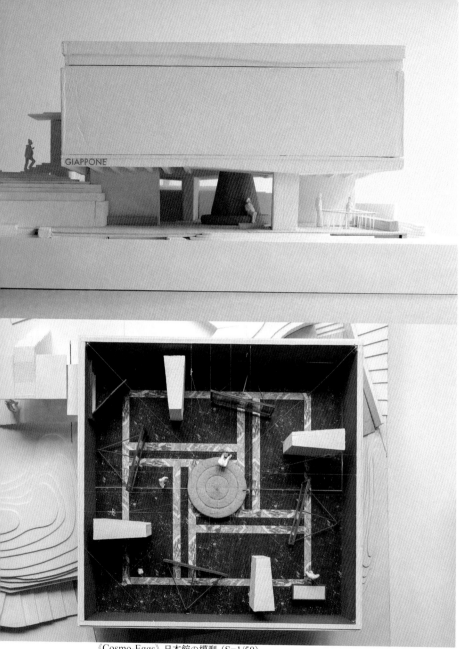

《Cosmo-Eggs》日本館の模型（S=1/50）
1/50 scale model of Japan Pavilion with *Cosmo-Eggs* exhibit

Background as
Tactile Experience

I participated in the *Cosmo-Eggs* exhibit, at the Japan Pavilion during the 2019 Venice Biennale International Art Exhibition, as part of an interdisciplinary team: artist Motoyuki Shitamichi, composer Taro Yasuno, anthropologist Toshiaki Ishikura, curator Hiroyuki Hattori, and myself. Shitamichi showed video works featuring tsunami boulders, large rocks from the seafloor swept ashore by tsunami during massive earthquakes; Yasuno staged a performer-less, fully automatic "zombie music" piece in which a balloon supplied the air pressure to play recorder flutes; Ishikura presented, in text form, egg-based creation myths collected during fieldwork in Okinawa, Taiwan and elsewhere. It struck me that I did not have portable works of my own to bring to the exhibit. The task of an architect is to deal with each request as it comes, based on various conditions, and I began wondering whether I had really been doing what I wanted to do in my career thus far. In the early stages of the project I was consulted about burying the Japan Pavilion[1] in soil, but I responded that I would like to work with the existing pavilion designed by Takamasa Yoshizaka[2]. As I thought it over, I came to believe that in my capacity as an architect, I could turn the Japan Pavilion exhibit design into a portable work in its own right.

The video works were shown using rear projection (projected from behind onto translucent film). As the projection distance needed to correspond to the sizes of the screens, I designed frame units that integrated projectors and screens, rendering visible the mechanism of projection. In light of the mobile nature of the tsunami boulders I attached wheels to the frames for mobility, and the movable screens were fitted between the Japan Pavilion's pillars, which are positioned in a spiraling formation, while all facing toward the center. The "zombie music" required an enormous balloon and blower to blow air through the recorder flutes, and the blower produced extraneous wind noise and vibrational noise. There is a hole in the center of the Japan Pavilion gallery floor that connects the gallery above and the piloti space below, and the blower was placed in the piloti space, the recorders in the gallery, and the balloon positioned so as to penetrate and block the hole, preventing noise from reaching the gallery. The

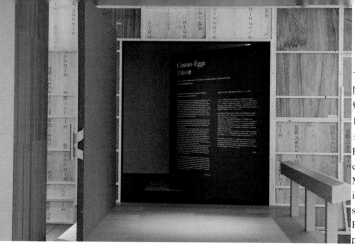

アーティゾン美術館にて
開催された《Cosmo-Eggs》
帰国展では90%サイズの
日本館再現模型がベニヤと
ダンボールで制作された
For the *Cosmo-Eggs*
exhibition at the Artizon
Museum in Japan, held after
its overseas run, a 90%-
size model of the Japanese
Pavilion was built with
plywood and cardboard

walls of the Japan Pavilion are painted pure white to achieve a bright interior, but here to make the images stand out they were painted the muddy green of a dim swamp, with luminosity provided by natural light from the skylight and the glow of the projections. The texts of creation myths were engraved directly into the wall, subtly revealing the white paint beneath and the texture of the underlying medium-density fiberboard.

According to unwritten rules of art appreciation, when viewing a painting, the viewer ignores the painting's frame and indeed the entire gallery space. Similarly, when we read a book, the information conveyed by the text occupies the foreground, and the paper and ink the background. These are examples of how human beings evidently follow rules dictating that we perceive objects and their environments separately. However, in *Cosmo-Eggs* the intent was for the background of gallery and frames to be integrated with the works when operating on viewers' perceptions. My role as architect was to push the environment, usually relegated to the subconscious, forward somewhat and generate a unique sensory experience. Backgrounds are not the focus of attention in the same manner as art objects or sculptures, but they are capable of fulfilling their function as backgrounds while presenting the viewer with a wondrous tactile experience.

Notes

1——The Japanese Pavilion at the Venice Biennale
The pavilion at the Giardini venue. Designed by Takamasa Yoshizaka, completed in 1956.

2——Takamasa Yoshizaka (1917–80)
One of Japan's most prominent architects, he studied under Le Corbusier and was a professor at Waseda University.

制約とやぶれかぶれ

建物は基本的に四角で構成されている。四角い部屋は家具が置きやすい、四角い窓は開け閉めしやすい、四角い建物はつくりやすい、それゆえお金がかからない。事務所でのスタディはできる限り四角い建物で進める。四角以外の形のスケッチが出てくると、何か間違ったことをしていないか点検する。他の建築と差別化するために四角以外の形が出てくると要注意である。どうしても四角よりも優れた形はある。そのひとつは屋根である。雨を流すために勾配が生じるからである。このように理に適った形以外は原則的に四角にこだわり、粘るようにしている。

　平面図よりも断面図を大事にする。平面図はクライアントの要望や使い方に沿っておおよそ決まってくる。奇を衒ったプランニングはときには住み手を不幸にしてしまう可能性がある。平面は建築家の表現の主戦場としてはいけない。対して、建物の高さ方向は要望や使い方からは決まらない。断面図には地面との関係、太陽との関係、周囲の建物との関係、構造や開口部などの情報が埋め込まれる。断面図には建物の仕組みが率直に表れている。私は特に短手の矩計図で考えるのが好きである。矩計図を見れば設計者の思考の痕跡がよくわかる。

　細部の納まりについても付け加えたい。建築家の作品のなかには幾何学的な形態を純粋に見せようとするために、ピン角、枠なし、チリなし、見切りなし、巾木なし、という細部のデザインをしばしば見かける。しかし材料が持っている物質性を捻じ曲げたり、施工し難いと修理しにくくなり、後々痛い目にあってしまう。そこで私は材料の性質や施工性に従って細部を検討する。こうした物質性や施工性に従うことは一見制約と感じるかもしれないが、物質の可能性を引き伸ばすともいえる。例えばDIYで珪藻土を塗ることが多いが、巾木がないと非常に塗りにくい。慣習的な細部には材料の性質とそれに従った施工のしやすさなど、さまざまな知恵が詰まっている。そうした先人の知恵を汲み取るのがむしろ楽しい。

材料の工業化やデジタル技術によって自由な形をつくること
が可能になった。しかしそこには際限がない。制約を解除して成立したデザインは自由気儘なことを表現しているにすぎない。制約を解除するデザインではなく、制約を発見するデザインのほうが好きである。プロジェクトのなかで何が制約なのか見極めて、プロジェクトのポテンシャルを最大限生かそうとするのである。そうすることで制約がプロジェクトの独自性を受け入れる下地になっていくのだ。

　例えば《馬込の平入》（2016）では、クライアントが用意した平面図を元に設計が進行した。限られた間口幅の敷地で風通しを良くするために私はその平面図に従いながら天井高を通常の1.5倍にした。コストを大幅に下げるために、ハウスメーカーが大量に仕入れている内装はプラスターボードにクロス貼り、外装はリシン吹き付け、屋根はガルバリウム鋼板といった標準仕様の

《馬込の平入》DIYで珪藻土塗り
DIY application of silica at *Hirairi in Magome*

材料を使った。既製品を使わないようにしてきた私にとっては辛い決断だったが、ほかに選択肢はなかった。しかしクライアントも私もビニルクロスが嫌いだったため、ビニルクロスを貼らずにプラスターボードのまま引き渡してもらうことにした。そこで家族や友人で珪藻土を塗ってみようと盛り上がった。天井が高いため、手の届く範囲を珪藻土、それより上はプラスターボード露わしの未完成のままとした。手作りと既製品と未完成の独特なハイブリッドになった。

《西大井のあな》（2019）では、建物を購入後すぐに改修の設計に取りかかり、3つの工務店に見積もりを依頼をした。しかし繁忙期だったためすべての工務店から断られてしまった（建築家夫婦の自宅のリノベーションは危険だと思われたのかもしれない）。別の工務店に見積もり依頼の準備を進め、設計案を修正しているうちに、引っ越しの時期が迫ってきてしまった。なんとか廃棄物や粉塵が出る解体だけは引っ越し前に終わらせたかった。そこで解体指示書のみ作成することになった。つまり解体がすなわち設計となったのだ。どこを解体すべきかを悩み、小さな面積で最も効果のある階段脇の廊下のスラブに「あな」を開けることに決めた。何とかギリギリに解体工事が終わり、引っ越しの日を迎えた。最初はひたすら掃除をする日々だった。こうして《西大井のあな》は自分たちの実験場になった。

　建築の面白さは形の自由さではない。それはプロジェクトの制約に向き合った結果得られる思いがけない発明や発見である。凡庸さに耐え忍び、その先にある「やぶれかぶれ」のアイデアからユニークな建築が生まれてくるのではないか。

Limitations and Desperation

Buildings are basically composed of rectangles. It is easy to arrange furniture in a rectangular room, rectangular windows are easy to open and close, rectangular buildings are easy to build and therefore cost-effective. When studies are conducted in my office, rectangular spaces are used whenever possible. If I see an architectural drawing containing a shape other than a rectangle, my instinct is to check and make sure nothing is wrong. At the same time, it is important to note that non-rectangular shapes are incorporated into buildings so as to differentiate them from others. There are certainly places where a rectangle is not the best shape, one of which is a roof, because rain creates the need for a gradient. In principle, though, I stick to rectangles except when there is a logical reason to do otherwise.

A cross-sectional view is more important than a floor plan. Floor plans are roughly determined according to clients' requests and intended usage, and innovative or even eccentric planning can run the risk of making residents unhappy. The primary battlefield of architectural expression should not be the floor plan. On the other hand, building heights are not determined by requests or intended usage. Embedded in the cross-sectional plan is information such as relationships with ground, sun, and surrounding buildings, and about the structure and its apertures. A cross-sectional view straight-forwardly shows the structure of a building. Personally, I especially like to reference sectional detail drawings, which give you a glimpse into the architect's thought process.

Here I would also like to discuss handling of details. Some architects frequently produce designs with detailing featuring pin angles and with no window or door frames, no partitions, no base-boards and so forth, so as to showcase pure geometric forms. However, if materials' properties are such that they bend or are difficult to work with, they will be difficult to repair and troubles will occur at a later date. For this reason, I plan details in light of the properties and workability of materials. Being governed by materiality and work-ability in this way may seem to be a limitation, but it can also be said to expand the potential of materials. For example, diatomaceous soil is often applied in DIY projects, but it is extremely difficult to apply if there is no baseboard. Such customary detailing practices

《西大井のあな》塗装と養生
Coating in progress and protective sheeting at
Holes in the House (Casa a Nishioi)

are abundant sources of knowledge, such as about the properties of materials and ease of workability based on these properties. When it comes to these matters it is, in fact, quite enjoyable to draw on the wisdom of our forebears.

Industrialization of materials and digital technologies have made it possible to design forms freely, but this means that there are no limitations. Designs produced without constraints are expressions of the freedom to do as one likes, no more and no less. However, I prefer designs that identify limitations rather than removing them. We endeavor to maximize the potential of a project by identifying what its constraints are. By doing so, limitations become the basis for acceptance of a project's unique features.

For example, the design for *Hirairi in Magome* (2016) (*hirairi* is a traditional Japanese structure with the main entrance on the side running parallel to the roof ridge) was carried out based on a floor plan prepared by the client. To improve ventilation on a site with limited frontage width, we increased ceiling height to 1.5 times the standard while adhering to the floor plan. To reduce costs significantly, we employed standard materials: for the interior plasterboard, which home builders procure in large quantities, covered with wallpaper; for the exterior lysine spray; for the roof Galvalume (aluminum-zinc alloy coated sheet steel). These were tough decisions, as I have tried

ロックウールの飛散を防止するために
表面を塗装で固める
Applying a surface coating so rock wool
does not scatter

to avoid using off-the-shelf products, but there were no other options. The client and I agreed that we dislike vinyl wallpaper, so we elected to leave the plasterboard as is. As a result, the client decided to make a fun DIY project out of applying diatomaceous soil with family and friends. Because of the high ceilings, the silica extends only as high as people could reach, and above that the plasterboard is left unfinished. The project is a unique hybrid of handmade, ready-made, and unfinished.

For *Holes in the House (Casa A Nishioi)* (2019), we began planning renovations immediately after purchasing the building, and asked three contractors for estimates. However, all of them refused as it was a busy season (and perhaps it seemed risky to renovate a house occupied by a husband and wife who are both architects). As we were preparing to request an estimate from yet another contractor, and amending the design proposal, the time to move in was approaching. We wanted at least to have the demolition, which produces debris and dust, finished before moving in. Thus, we decided to prepare only instructions for what to dismantle, and this in effect became the design. After pondering which parts should be dismantled, we decided to open "holes" in the slabs in corridors next to the stairs, so as to use the small area most effectively. When moving day came, the demolition had just barely been completed, and the first order of business was to clean up. *Holes in the House (Casa A Nishioi)* had become our own experimental site as well as a residence.

The joy of architecture lies not in formal freedom, but in unexpected inventions and discoveries that emerge from engagement with projects' limitations. I believe that unique architecture emerges from embracing the mediocrity of existing conditions, and building on inspiration born of desperation.

物質循環のネットワーク

　建築は物質からできている。物質は多面的に解釈されうる。物質を構造的・力学的に捉えることもできれば、有用か無用かという道具的な解釈をすることもでき、素材感という感覚的な側面からも捉えることができる。あるいは空間を形づくる部品としても捉えることができる。私は物質を流れや循環のなかで捉えたいと思う。

　建築材料は物質であるとともに人間世界が内蔵されている。例えば製材された木材と技術者である大工は互いに結びついている。技術だけではなく、法律、流通、経済などとも固く結びついている。建築の各要素の履歴に着目すると、建築要素−製品−加工−原料−資源というように下流から上流に遡れば最終的には自然の資源に辿り着く。さらに建築が使われなくなれば、解体されて廃棄される。一部の物質は再利用や再循環の過程に入るが、それ以外は燃やされて埋め立てられる。こうした物質循環を把握することは生態学的には重要だが、設計の際に意識に上ることが少ない。なぜなら物質が資源という上流から現場という下流へと流れるのに対し、需要に関する情報は消費者のいる下流から逆方向に流れていくため、消費者に近い都合の良い情報だけが開示され、それ以外の情報はブラックボックス化されているからである。消費者が選択できるのはカタログやネットで閲覧することができる製品までで、その物質が誰によって、どのように、どこでつくられているのかわかりにくくなっている。設計者は限定されたネットワークのなかで創作することになり、その結果、建築は既製品を組み合わせる範囲内での形態やイメージの創出に偏っていくことになる。

　まず、建築がどのようなネットワークに取り囲まれているかを認識することが大事である。ブラックボックスを開示することによりネットワークの善し悪しが判断できるようになり、より良いネットワークを繋ぎ直していくことができる。しかしそれは簡単なことではなく、コスト、工期、人手の問題に直面す

る。巨大な産業によって経済優先の物質循環のネットワークが整備されているため、そのネットワークを直ちに変更することは極めて困難である。しかし設計者はこうした物のネットワークを「見える化」することから始めなければならないだろう。

　このような建築から資源への物質循環のネットワークを、建築を中心に資源を周囲に配置して図式化する。産業社会の枠組みのなかでは、法律や条例あるいは生産−消費の流通システムが整備されていることで資源と建築との間に障壁が存在している。専門家や企業の開発部などの会議体によって意思決定され、産業システムが構築されているためである。この図式は「障壁モデル」と呼べるだろう。

　　これに対し、障壁を取り払うか、弱めるか、すり抜けるかのいくつかの選択肢がある。障壁自体に働きかけるためには、専門家として意見するか、制度を見直すように促すことが可能であるが、個別の建築の設計では障壁をすり抜けるように、資源へのアクセシビリティを確保することが現実的だろう。例えば

《高岡のゲストハウス》プロセス模型
Process model of *Takaoka Guest House*

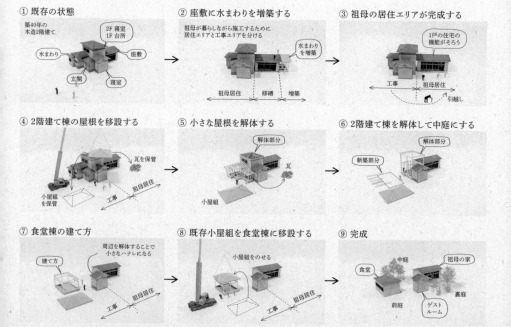

① 既存の状態

築40年の木造2階建て
2F 寝室
1F 台所
水まわり
座敷
玄関
寝室

② 座敷に水まわりを増築する

祖母が暮らしながら施工するために居住エリアと工事エリアを分ける
水まわりを増築
祖母居住　修繕　増築

③ 祖母の居住エリアが完成する

1戸の住宅の機能がそろう
工事　祖母居住
引越し

④ 2階建て棟の屋根を移設する

瓦を保管
小屋組を保管　工事　祖母居住

⑤ 小さな屋根を解体する

解体部分
瓦
小屋組

⑥ 2階建て棟を解体して中庭にする

解体部分
新築部分

⑦ 食堂棟の建て方

周辺を解体することで小さなハナレになる
建て方
工事　祖母居住

⑧ 既存小屋組を食堂棟に移設する

小屋組をのせる
工事　祖母居住

⑨ 完成

中庭　祖母の家
食堂
裏庭
前庭　ゲストルーム

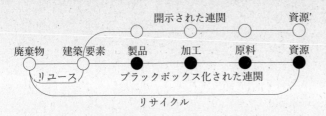

建築の物質循環の模式図
Schematic diagram of material
circulation in architecture

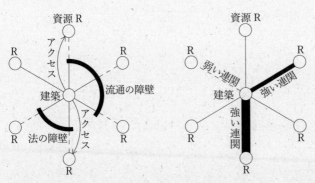

左：物質循環の障壁モデル
右：物質循環の運河モデル
Left: "Barrier model" of
material circulation
Right: "Channel model" of
material circulation

　裏山の樹木を建材に使いたい場合には、一般的に流通している機械乾燥されて含水率が低い木材とは異なり、長い時間をかけて自然乾燥をしたり、より強度のある大断面の木材を使用することなどが挙げられる。

　また大企業の製品と地域のものづくりを比較すると、ネットワークの質がまったく異なっている。前者は法や流通などを味方につけた上流から下流に向けた巨大な流れであるのに対し、後者は顔の見える人に届く分だけの細々とした流れである。こうした物質循環の運河が消費者に向かって整備されているが、多くの消費者は大企業のネットワークを好む傾向がある。そうした好みには、コスト、信用、社会通念などが絡み合っている。この図式は「運河モデル」と呼べるだろう。

　これに対して、適切なネットワークを選択することが効果的である。それは投票と似ている。物を選ぶことは物質循環のネットワークを選ぶことである。消費者の行動が変われば、上流のあり方も変わるのである。設計者は消費者の代理でもあるため、ネットワークの選択に責任を持たなければいけない。

　次に建築が使われなくなり廃棄される際の物質循環の流れについて考えてみる。今度は建築が上流で廃棄物が下流となる。建築はさまざまな物質によって構成されているため、それぞれ

の物質の性質によって処理の方法は異なっている。再利用（リ
ユース）、再循環（リサイクル）、生分解、燃焼、埋め立てなど
である。まず廃棄物の総量を減らすためには建物を長く使うこ
とが大事である。そのため建築の長寿命化を目指さなければな
らないが、問題は物質の耐久性というよりは激しい社会変化へ
の対応、新品に価値を置く文化の影響が大きいだろう。また再
利用や再循環をさせるためにはゴミの分別のように建築材料が
分別可能に構築されていないといけない。環境汚染を引き起こ
さないように生分解可能な物質で構成することも大事である。

このような物質循環を真剣に受け止めることはデザインの足枷
になるだろうか。私は物質循環への配慮が創作上の障害ではな
く、むしろ建築に新しい生態学的転回をもたらすのではないか
と考えている。既製品のような予測可能な物質を扱えば設計は
スムーズに進行する。しかし既製品とは異なるネットワークか
ら届けられる物質は、ときにはゴツゴツして扱いにくいが、事
物連関への感覚を広げてくれる。こうした独自のネットワーク
に繋ぎ直されることで物質の構成法も修正される。それは物質
が形態に従属しているのではなく、物質の系と形態の系が衝突
しあう、新しい建築の方法となるはずだ。

Material Circulation Networks

Buildings consist of materials, and materials can be interpreted in various ways. They can be regarded as structure or strength of materials; they can be interpreted as tools, in terms of their usefulness or lack thereof; they can be grasped in terms of sensory qualities such as texture. Or, they can be regarded as components that make up a space. Personally, I seek to interpret materials in terms of flow and circulation.

Construction materials are pieces of matter, and at the same time they are imbued with aspects of the human world. For example, sawn timbers and the carpenters who process them are inextricably connected, not only in terms of artisanal expertise but also of law, logistics, economics and so forth. If we look at the history of each element of a building, working backward from downstream to upstream, we progress from architectural element, to product, to processing, to raw material, and finally arrive at natural resource. When a building is no longer useful, it is demolished and the materials disposed of. Some go into the cycle of reuse and recirculation, while others are burned or sent to landfills. From an ecological standpoint it is important to understand this material cycle, but architects are rarely conscious of it during the design process. This is because materials flow from upstream (resources) to downstream (construction site), while information about demand for designs flows in the opposite direction, starting downstream (consumers). This means that only information familiar and relevant to consumers is disclosed, the rest stored in a metaphorical black box. Consumers can only select products viewable in catalogs or online, making it difficult to tell how, where, and by whom a material is made. Architects work within limited networks, and as a result, architecture is biased toward creating forms and images within the scope of combinations of ready-made products.

It is important, first of all, that we recognize the nature of the network to which architecture connects. Opening the black box makes it possible to judge the network on its merits and demerits, and to rewire it as something more positive. However, this is no easy task and there are challenges in terms of cost, construction, and workforce. It is extremely difficult to alter the network quickly, because a massive industry has established a network of material cycles that prioritizes economics above all. Nonetheless, architects need to begin by rendering this network visible.

This network of material cycles, from building to resources and back again, can be rendered visible schematically by placing construction at the center with resources arranged around it. Within the framework of an industrial society, there are barriers between resources and construction due to systems of laws and regulations, and the logistical system of production-consumption. This is because the industrial system is structured through decisions made in groups, such as panels of experts or companies' development divisions. This schema could be described as the "barrier model."

However, there are several options for removing, weakening, or slipping through the cracks of these barriers. To impact the barriers themselves, experts can state opinions or urge that the system be updated, but in enabling individual architectural designs to bypass barriers, a more realistic approach is to ensure accessibility to resources on a case-by-case basis. An example is use of wood: if one wants to use trees from a nearby mountain as building materials, one can allow their wood to dry naturally over a long period of time and have access to stronger, thicker timbers, as opposed to using machine-dried wood with low moisture content that is generally commercially available.

When major companies' products are compared with those

左：第15回ヴェネチア・ビエンナーレ国際建築展
日本館展示（2016）
右：《高岡のゲストハウス》模型（S=1/30）とマテリアルの実物
Left: Japan Pavilion exhibit at the 15th Venice Biennale International Architecture Exhibition (2016)
Right: 1/30 scale model of *Takaoka Guest House* and actual material sample

of local manufacturers, the qualities of the networks involved are completely different. The former is a massive flow from upstream to downstream, with legal and logistical systems on its side, while the latter is a small flow extending only to people who meet face to face. In both cases the channels of material cycles flow toward consumers, but many consumers tend to prefer large corporate networks. These preferences are entangled with issues of cost, credibility, and social consensus. This schema can be described as the "channel model."

But selecting the appropriate network is an effective means of achieving positive outcomes, analogous to voting in an election. When we select a product or material, we select a network of material cycles. If consumer behavior changes, the way things operate upstream will change as well. One of architects' roles is to act on behalf of consumers, and they must be responsible for network selection.

Next, let us consider the flow of the material cycle when buildings are no longer used and are disposed of. Now things are reversed, the building is upstream and the waste products are downstream. Buildings are composed of various materials, and each material is handled differently depending on its properties: reused, recycled, biodegraded, incinerated, sent to landfills and so forth. First of all it is vital that we lengthen the lifespans of buildings so as to reduce the total amount of waste. To extend lifespans, the issue is not so much durability of materials as it is buildings' adaptability to drastic social changes, and the influence of consumer culture that glorifies the new. Also, to reuse and recycle materials, buildings must be constructed so that they can be separated, just as household garbage is separated into categories. It is also important to maximize use of biodegradable substances so as not to pollute the environment.

Do we shackle architects when we ask them to take these material cycles seriously? I believe that considering material cycles does not act as a creative constraint, but rather brings architecture into a new ecosystemic mode. Architectural design goes smoothly when predictable materials such as off-the-shelf products are used. However, while materials delivered through other networks than these off-the-shelf products are sometimes rugged and difficult to handle, they expand our sense of connections among things, and reconnecting to unique networks can improve our choices of materials to use. The result ought to be a new approach to architecture in which material and form collide and intersect, rather than material being subordinate to form.

分解派建築

自然界には生産者、消費者、分解者が存在する。光合成によって自ら栄養をつくりだす植物が「生産者」、植物を食べる草食動物やそれを食べる肉食動物などが「消費者」、そしてそれらの糞や死骸を食べる微生物などが「分解者」である。土壌や海水中にいる多くの微生物は、有機物を水や二酸化炭素やアンモニアなどの無機物に分解する。

　建設産業には生産−消費−廃棄という物質循環がある。自然界には「廃棄」ではなく「分解」のみがある。人工物の世界にはゴミが存在し、自然界の循環システムにはゴミが存在しない。自然界の循環のなかにある生物的代謝はバイオスフィアと呼ばれ、人工物の循環のなかにある技術的代謝はテクノスフィアと呼ばれている。

　建築を生物的代謝（バイオスフィア）のなかだけでつくることができれば、それは最良の手段である。植物のような生分解する物質のみでつくられる建築である。しかし人間は古代から鉄やコンクリートやガラスという化学変化させた物質をつくりだし、私たちの生活を進展させてきた。こうした人工物は少量であれば、地球環境や生態系に対するインパクトは小さいのかもしれないが、世界全体の人間が廃棄する人工物は深刻なダメージを地球に与えることになる。そこでテクノスフィアでは人工物が完全にリサイクルされることが目標とされている。しかしペットボトルなどもリサイクル素材として開発されたにもかかわらず、リサイクルする際に内容物の汚れの洗浄やシールを剥がす手間を要する。またペットボトルが置き去りにされると土埃と混ざってしまう。プラスチックが純粋な状態で回収されればいいのだが、さまざまな汚れが混入する。プラスチックが磨耗することで目に見えないほど粉々の状態になり、排水されて海に流されてしまう。この海に浮遊するマイクロプラスチックに汚染物質が付着し魚が食べ、人間がその魚を食べるという循環が起きている。このようにバイオスフィアとテクノスフィア

が混在することにより、互いの循環を汚染し合っている。生物代謝と技術的代謝は完全に分離されていなくてはならない。

　建築はさまざまな物質を組み合わせてつくられる。だからこそ建築はバイオスフィアとテクノスフィアを分離できるようにあらかじめデザインされていないといけない。そうした分離可能なデザインはまだ途上であるが、簡単に自分なりの方向を示したい。まず建築はできる限り生分解可能なバイオスフィアの循環のなかでつくられることが目指されるべきである。例えば木や藁や竹や紙などの植物素材、あるは土や石などの素材で建築がつくられるべきである。そのなかでも建物の雨の影響を受けやすい部分や腐食が早い部分である屋根や窓や水まわりには完全に分離可能なテクノスフィアを用いてもいいだろう。屋根には100%リサイクル可能な金属系の材料、窓にはリサイクル可能なガラスを用いる。水まわりについてはユニットバスやシンクやトイレなどの乾式のパーツで建築と簡易に着脱可能にする。地域資源の植物や土や石をオンサイトで制作する建築本体と、完全分離・再循環可能なレディメイドの製品の組み合わせが、分解される建築の仕組みになるだろう。

20世紀に人類は急激な都市化を経験した。物質の側から見れば、鉄、アルミ、ガラス、コンクリート、木材といった物質が都市に集中したとも言い換えられる。鉄やアルミはほぼ100%リサイクルが可能で、木材は燃料になる。コンクリートはリサイクルは難しいが砕石になる。そうした視点で都市を観てみると、例えば鉄骨のビルは鉄の貯蔵庫、アルミサッシの反復するビルはアルミの貯蔵庫に見えてくる。急成長して朽ち始めた都市をリサイクル可能なマテリアルで満たされた貯蔵庫とポジティ

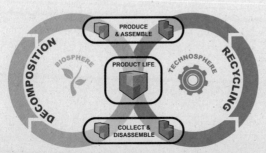

生物的代謝と技術的代謝の模式図
Schematic diagram of biological metabolism and technological metabolism

引用出典／References =
https://medium.com/@bluehair.
co/cradle-to-cradle-hype-or-hope-
27948eea7bc6

ブに捉え直すこともできるはずである。建築することが都市に
堆積した人工物を循環させていく手段としても捉えることがで
きるだろう。

　建物の廃棄物を少なくするためには、建物の寿命に対する新た
な考え方も必要だ。例えば生分解可能な素材でできた建築は10
〜20年くらいで朽ちてもいいと考えてみる。空き家になっても
無理なくすっきり土に戻る建築である。現代人はそれぞれのラ
イフステージに応じて頻繁に引っ越し、家を売買して、居を移
していくことを考えれば、分解可能な家を安く素人でも簡単に
建てられてもいいのではないか。そのためには建物の材料を土
に還す分解地が必要である。こうした短寿命の建築に対して高
いエネルギーと超耐久性のあるマテリアルを費やしてつくられる
1,000年を超える長寿命の建築も同時にあるといい。例えば、歴
史的建造物やモニュメント、公共的な建物などである。この長
寿命の建築と短寿命の生分解の建築が組み合わさることで、都
市のなかに異なった時間性を有する建築群が並存していくので
ある。10年スパンで分解される流動的領域と腐敗を促進する分
解地、そして1,000年を超える建造物が残る歴史的領域が相互
に依存しあうのである。

　　現在の建物はメンテナンスフリーで楽をしようという魂胆
でできている。そこには分解や腐敗の概念がなく、新品状態を
維持することを求めて無理をしている。使わなくなれば壊して
再開発するという使い捨ての建築の考え方が経済を回している。
しかし土壌と共存しなければ都市は徐々に衰微し、崩壊する運
命にある。私たちは土壌とともに生きる存在なのである。私た
ちの居住地は土壌の力を借りた分解都市となるべきだ。次の千
年紀を生き延びるためには、土壌の分解と腐敗を基盤にした都
市文明のヴィジョンが必要なのだ。

参考文献
- 藤原辰史『分解の哲学——腐敗と発酵をめぐる思考』(青土社、2019)
- マイケル・ブラウンガード + ウィリアム・マクダナー『サスティナブルなもの
　づくり——ゆりかごからゆりかごへ』(岡山慶子 + 吉村英子監修、山本聡 + 山
　崎正人訳、人間と歴史社、2009)

Decompositional Architecture

In the natural world, there are producers, consumers, and decomposers. Plants that manufacture nutrients through photosynthesis are producers, herbivores that eat plants and carnivores that eat the herbivores are consumers, and microorganisms that consume feces and carcasses are decomposers. Countless microorganisms in the soil and seawater decompose organic matter into inorganic substances such as water, carbon dioxide and ammonia.

The construction industry has a material flow of production-consumption-disposal. In the natural world, however, there is no disposal, only decomposition. In the world of human-made objects there is such a thing as garbage, but there is no garbage in the

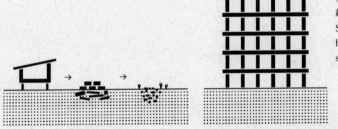

分解短寿命建築と
超耐久超寿命建築
Short-lived biodegradable
building and ultra-durable,
super-long-lasting building

cycle of nature. The natural cycle's biological metabolism is known as the biosphere, and the artificial cycle's technological metabolism can be called the "technosphere."

Ideally, buildings could be constructed solely from the biosphere. This would mean architecture employing only biodegradable materials, such as plant matter. However, since ancient times human beings have been producing chemically altered materials such as iron, concrete, and glass that have improved our lifestyles. In small amounts, human-made materials may have only a small impact on the global environment and local ecosystems, but the totality of these materials disposed of worldwide causes tremendous damage to the planet. Thus, the goal in the technosphere is eventually to recycle all human-made materials. However, while plastic bottles, to give one example, were developed as recyclable materials, it takes time to clean out their contents and remove their stickers during recycling, and they are often discarded as litter or soiled by other garbage. Plastic needs to be collected in a pure state for recycling, but in reality it is compromised by all manner of other waste, and as plastic deteriorates it gets crushed into pieces too small to be seen and drained off, ending up in the ocean. A cycle has emerged in which pollutants adhere to microplastics suspended in the ocean, fish consume the microplastics, and humans consume the fish. Biosphere and technosphere mix, each contaminating the cycle of the other. The biological and technological metabolisms need to be thoroughly separated.

Architectural structures are combinations of a variety of materials, and must be pre-designed to separate biosphere and technosphere. The development of separable designs like these is still in progress, but here I would like to briefly outline my own ideas. First, architecture should aim for construction of buildings within the cycle of the biosphere to the greatest possible extent. For example, buildings should be constructed with biodegradable, plant-derived materials like wood, straw, bamboo and paper, or natural materials like earth and stone. Within this framework, completely separable technosphere materials can be used for roofs, windows, and plumbing-related areas that are vulnerable to rain and corrode easily: 100% recyclable metal for roofs, recyclable glass for windows. As for water-adjacent areas, essentially dry sections such as unit baths, sinks, and toilets should be easily removable from buildings. The mechanism of a decomposable building is a combination of a building produced on-site, from local resources such as plants, soil and stone, and ready-made products that can be completely detached and recycled.

In the 20th century, humankind experienced rapid urbanization, and in material terms we saw a concentration in cities of materials such as iron, aluminum, glass, concrete, and wood. Iron and aluminum can be almost completely recycled, and wood can be reused as fuel. Concrete is difficult to recycle, but it can be turned into crushed stone. When we look at a city from this perspective, a steel-frame building looks like an iron mine, and a building with rows of aluminum-sash windows looks like an aluminum mine. A fast-growing, quickly decaying city can be positively viewed as a treasure trove of recyclable materials. Constructing buildings can be seen as a means of circulating human-made materials that accumulate in the city, and architects can become the decomposers in the metabolism of the technosphere.

To reduce waste from buildings, we need new ways of thinking about their lifespans. For example, if we have a building consisting of biodegradable material, there is no problem with it falling apart in 10 to 20 years. If a house like this becomes vacant, it will fully and smoothly revert to the soil. Considering that people today move frequently, buy and sell homes, and relocate according to their life stage, what if people had access to biodegradable houses that even an amateur can easily construct? This would necessitate decomposition sites where the building materials would return to the earth. In contrast to these short-lived buildings, there is also a need for structures that last over a thousand years, which would be built with highly energy-intensive, ultra-durable materials. Examples include historic buildings, monuments, and public facilities. With a combination of super-long-lasting buildings and short-lived biodegradable ones, cities would contain groups of structures that exist on different timelines. There would be dynamically shifting areas home to buildings that decompose in a 10-year span, decomposition sites where conditions enable structures to decay rapidly, and historic districts where buildings over a thousand years old remain, all coexisting in a symbiotic relationship.

In current construction practices there is an ulterior motive, to make buildings maintenance-free and user-friendly. No thought is given to the eventual disassembly and decomposition of structures, and architects stretch the limits so as to design buildings that stay in brand-new condition. The mindset of disposable architecture – when a building falls into disuse, demolish it and build a new one – acts as an economic driver. However, if cities do not start coexisting with the soil, they are destined to gradually decline and collapse. We are organisms that coexist with soil, and we should live in communities that biodegrade with soil's help. If we are to survive over the coming millennium, what we need is a vision of urban civilization grounded in soil's properties of decomposition and decay.

References
- Tatsushi Fujihara, *The Philosophy of Decomposition: Thoughts on Decay and Fermentation*, Seidosha, 2019.
- Michael Braungart & William McDonough, *Cradle to Cradle: Remaking the Way We Make Things* (translated by Yamamoto Satoshi and Yamazaki Masato, editorial supervision by Okayama Keiko and Yoshimura Hideko), Ningen to Rekishi-sha, 2009.

屋根の移動

《高岡のゲストハウス》（2016）は、築40年の木造家屋を、私の祖母の住まいと家族や友人が宿泊できるゲストハウスへと改修する計画だ。この家には、祖父母、父母、子どもの3世代が住んでいたが、今は祖母がひとりで住んでいる。ひとりの住まいにしては広すぎるため、家の一部を食堂やゲストルームにつくりかえて、家族や友人が集まれる場所にする。既存の建物を壊して新築するのではなく、部分的に解体しては段階的に修繕をするという計画である。

　計画地は、瓦屋根の古い住宅、建て売りの新興住宅、所々に残された水田が入り混じった、田舎の住宅地のありきたりな風景のなかにある。周辺の建物は、壁はトタンやサイディング、窓はアルミサッシで、その多くの屋根には瓦が葺かれている。そのなかでも、瓦屋根はこの場所にとってはありきたりな建築の要素であるが、地域で共有された要素でもある。もし建築家がこの場所で新しい空間イメージを造形しようとするならば、瓦屋根は邪魔なものでしかないかもしれない。しかし、ありきたりなものほど地域の風景にとって価値のある要素になる。

　祖父母は高岡の伝統産業である銅器製造を生業としていたため、家には銅製の火鉢、香炉、文鎮、置物などが残されている。さらに座敷にある木彫が施された欄間や雪見障子は、家族にとっては懐かしいものである。既存の塀や外壁、土間に使わ

《高岡のゲストハウス》周辺の街並み
View of area around *Takaoka Guest House*

上：《高岡のゲストハウス》食堂
下：座敷の欄間と障子
Top: *Takaoka Guest House* dining room
Bottom: Transoms and *shoji* screens in the
tatami-floored room

れていたタイルや石なども庭の舗装として再利用する。新品の
建物を望むならば、これらは古臭くて、ノスタルジックすぎる
かもしれない。しかし家に残された銅器は高岡の町の伝統産業
を、欄間や雪見障子、庭は家族の記憶を生き生きと語る要素と
なるのである。これらを廃棄するのではなく、引き継いでいく
ことが、歴史や時間のなかに私たちが生きていることを感じさ
せるはずである。

　祖母が引越しをしないですむように、住みながら施工する
ために工事をいくつかの段階に分けることにした。そのことで
解体したマテリアルを再利用して次の建設資材として使い、敷
地内で生じるマテリアルの移動によって建築をつくることがで
きると気づいた。具体的な建設のプロセスを以下のように考え
た。第1期工事では既存の座敷に水まわりを増築して祖母の住
まいにし、第2期では2階建て部分を解体し、既存の瓦小屋組を
クレーンで吊り上げて新築の壁の上に移設し、既存の瓦を貼り

庭に保管された小屋組は
新築されたフレームに
載せられた
Storehouses in the garden
were mounted on newly
built frames

直す。第3期では寝室をゲストルームに改装し、第4期では既存
のマテリアルを再利用して庭を整備する。

　　建設プロセスのなかで小屋組の移設が最も祝祭的な場面
だった。部材を一つひとつ解体して組み直すとコストと工期が
かかる。寄棟屋根の四周の軒は火打梁で固定されているため小
屋組の平面形が矩形のまま保持される。そこでクレーンで吊り
上げる方法を採用することにした。建築は地に着いた不動のも
のであるイメージがあるため、屋根が空中に浮いた様子を想像
するだけで心躍るようだった。屋根がダイナミックに動くこと
で古い家屋に新鮮な生命感を吹き込める。小屋組と接合した柱
の頭部をチェンソーで切断し、屋根の四つ角と棟木の2カ所の合
計6カ所を固定して吊り上げた。クレーン作業は15分ほど。ま
るで凧揚げのように小屋組が浮いている姿はお祭りのようだっ
た。移動された小屋組はブルーシートを張って庭に保管された。
小屋組を採寸して、食堂の基礎の大きさを決定した。食堂の建
て方では雪のなか、小屋組が再度クレーンで吊り上げられ、ボ
ルトで梁に固定された。その後、屋根の下地と防水を新しくし
て、保管された瓦が葺き直された。3棟の建物が完成するとお
寺の境内の小さなお堂と蔵があるような静けさに包まれた。

Raising the Roof

The plan for *Guest House in Takaoka* (2016) was to convert a 40-year-old wood-frame house into a guest house where my grandmother would live and where family and friends would be able to stay. Three generations (grandparents, parents, and children) once lived in this house, but now my grandmother lives alone. It is too large for one person, so the idea was to convert part of the house into a dining room and guest rooms, where family and friends could assemble. The plan was not to demolish the existing building and build a new one, but to partially dismantle and reconstruct it in stages.

The site is in a typical rural residential area with old tiled-roof houses, new ready-built houses, and rice paddies remaining here and there. The surrounding buildings have walls of galvanized iron or vinyl siding, their windows are of the aluminum sash type, and many roofs are covered with traditional tiles. Among these architectural elements, tiled roofs are particularly common in this neighborhood, and also widespread throughout the area. If an architect wants to create an innovative spatial image in a location like this, a tiled roof might merely be an obstacle. However, the more common an ele-

第1期工事後の様子。左は既存家屋、右は改修された祖母の住まい
After the first phase of construction. On the left is the pre-existing house, and on the right is my grandmother's house after renovation.

《高岡のゲストハウス》中庭
Takaoka Guest House courtyard

ment is, the more vital it is to the local landscape.

My grandparents' business was making copperware, a traditional industry in Takaoka, and there are still copper cooking pots, incense burners, paperweights, and decorative objects around the house. The carved-wood transoms and vertically sliding shoji screens in the tatami-floored room evoke nostalgia for our family. The existing fence, outer wall, and tiles and stones in the earthen-floored space were reused as garden paving. If someone was trying for a slick, brand-new building, these things might be too old-fashioned and backward. But the copperware items left in the house that speak eloquently of the community's traditional industry, and the transoms, shoji screens, and garden are elements that vividly convey family memories. Inheriting rather than discarding them makes us feel that we are part of the flow of time and history.

We decided to divide construction into several stages so my grandmother would not have to move. As a result, we came to the realization that dismantled materials could be reused for new building, and a structure could be created through relocation of materials generated on the premises. The specific construction process we considered was as follows: In the first phase, bathroom, toilet, and kitchen were added onto an existing tatami-floored room to make it a residence for my grandmother. In the second phase, the two-story section of the building was dismantled and an existing roof framework (a tiled roof with all its beams and struts attached) was lifted with a crane and placed on top of newly built walls, with the same roof tiles reapplied. In the third phase, the bedroom was converted into a guest room, and in the fourth phase, materials already on site were reused to improve the garden.

The relocation of the roof framework was the most festive part of the construction process, though disassembling and reassembling the components one by one was both costly and time-consuming. As the eaves on the four sides of the hipped roof were fixed with diagonal braces, the original rectangular floor plan of the building had to be maintained, and we decided lifting it with a crane was the best approach. One thinks of structures like these as being immovable and fixed to the ground, so it was exciting just to imagine the roof floating in the air. Dynamic movement of a roof seems to breathe fresh life into an old house. The tops of columns connected to the roof framework were cut with a chainsaw, and the roof was attached to a crane at six locations (the four corners of the roof and two points on the roof ridge). The crane took about 15 minutes to do its work, and the structure floating in the air was a festive sight reminiscent of kite-flying. The relocated roof framework was stored in the garden, wrapped with a blue tarp. The dimensions of the dining room's foundation were determined by measuring the roof framework. During construction of the dining room a crane lifted the roof framework again, amid the snow, and bolted it to the beams of the new structure. After this the roof base and waterproofing were redone, and the stored roof tiles were reapplied. When the three buildings making up the guest house were completed, it had a serene atmosphere like the small sacred halls and storehouses on the grounds of a temple.

都市の土壌化と堆肥化

土壌は生命の基盤である。土のなかには目に見えない小さな微生物が豊富に存在している。植物の根のまわりには微生物の菌糸がネットワーク状に張り巡らされていて、植物と微生物の栄養となる有機化合物が双方向に流れている。菌糸が張り巡らされた土壌は団粒の構造になる。多数の団粒の隙間を通して新鮮な水と空気が行き届くことで植物は深く根を張ることができる。このように健全な土壌環境では根と菌糸と土が絡み合い頑丈になる。しかしコンクリートで土が分断されたり覆い被さってしまえば、菌糸による土の団粒構造は崩れ、水や空気の行き場がなく滞ってしまい、深く根を張る木々は衰えてしまう。このように微生物は土の健全性を保ってくれている重要なアクターである。

左：《西大井のあな》
コンクリート土間の削り
右：大量のコンクリートガラ
Left: Removing concrete to expose soil at *Holes in the House (Casa a Nishioi)*
Right: A large quantity of concrete fragments

　　こうした土のなかの微生物のことを考えると、コンクリートやアスファルトで覆われた都市は衰えた土の上に存在しているといえる。例えば、建物の基礎を最小限にして地表に土壌を取り返す。自動車のためのアスファルトではなく、微生物のための呼吸する地表にする。そうした建築や都市のビジョンが土壌生態学の視点から出てくるのではないか。

土を掘り返している様子
Digging up and turning over soil

　　土壌の微生物にとって大事な糞尿や生ゴミについても考えるべきだろう。水洗式のトイレに流された糞尿は下水を流れ、下水処理場で微生物によって分解され、その後塩素などによって消毒されて海に放流されている。生ゴミは燃えるゴミとして清掃工場で燃やされて灰になる。生ゴミは水分を多く含むため、燃やすために余計なエネルギーがかかってしまう。これらの糞尿や生ゴミをすべて廃棄物として処理するのではなく、その一部を土壌に返していくことも大事になってくる。土壌から都市を考え直すならば、まずはそれぞれの家に土を確保する必要があるだろう。そうすれば小さな庭で糞尿や生ゴミは分解され、庭どうしが菌糸によって繋がれ、植物の根から伸びた栄養や水のネットワークができるかもしれない。

　　《西大井のあな》の自宅兼事務所にはコンクリートで舗装された小さな駐車場があった。自動車を持っていない私たちにとって駐車場は必要ない。そこでコンクリートをスタッフやインターンと一緒に少しずつ削り、土壌が現れるようにした。コンクリートの大量のガラに圧倒された。土のなかには砕石やモルタルの細かな断片が混じり、ミミズやダンゴムシもいない死んだ土の状態だった。まず土壌を健康な状態にすることを目標にし

左：土壌に放たれたミミズ
右：落ち葉に生えた菌糸
Left: Earthworms released into the soil
Right: Fungus growing on fallen leaves

た。新鮮な空気を土のなかに送り込むために、土を掘り返し撹拌した。庭の端に溝を掘り、竹炭の粉末を入れ、その上に砕石、枯れ枝を敷き並べて、水の通り道にした。竹炭は多孔質構造で脱臭剤としても使われているが、水や空気を土壌に入り込みやすくする働きがある。コナラとモミジをいただいたので、竹炭と腐葉土を入れて植樹した。またダンボールの容器にピートモスとくん炭を混ぜてつくった自家製コンポストに、野菜屑などの生ゴミを入れて2カ月ほど熟成させ、庭の土に入れた。ミミズももらってきてこの庭に住んでもらった。1年くらい経って、雑草が生えてダンゴムシやアリやコオロギのいる庭になった。タンポポやハコベラなどの雑草、コンポストのなかに潜んでいた種子からは、カボチャ、ミニトマト、サツマイモが生えてきた。ある雑草が庭を覆ったかと思えば、枯れて腐食していき、別の草花が隆盛する。季節ごとに庭の植生がガラッと変化していく。これらは小さな庭の領土を巡って競争をしているようにも共存しているようにも見える。生命とはそういうものなのかもしれない。草花や樹木、小さな虫や目に見えない微生物が息づくことで、私たちは日々生命について学んでいる。たった一台分の狭い駐車場が土の庭になり、何倍もの広さと深さを感じるようになった。

参考文献
- 高田宏臣『土中環境——忘れられた共生のまなざし、蘇る古の技』(建築資料研究社、2020)
- デイビッド・モントゴメリー＋アン・ビクレー『土と内臓——微生物がつくる世界』(片岡夏実訳、築地書館、2016)

Urban Soil Conversion and Composting

Soil is the foundation of life. The ground below us teems with tiny, invisible microorganisms. The roots of plants are surrounded by mycelia (networks of thread-like fungi), and organic compounds flow back and forth between plants and the soil's microbiome, nourishing both. Soil pervaded by mycelia has a granular-unit structure, and plants are able to send their roots deep into the soil because fresh water and air penetrates the gaps between these countless granular units. In a healthy soil environment, roots, mycelia and soil intertwine to form a resilient, integrated system. However, when soil is sectioned off or covered with concrete, the granular-unit structure formed by mycelia collapses, there are no pathways for water and air to pass through, and trees with deep roots wither away. For this reason, microorganisms are crucial actors that maintain the health of the soil.

コナラ、モミジの苗木に水やり
Watering oak and Japanese maple saplings

《西大井のあな》2020年初夏の庭の様子
The garden at *Holes in the House*
(Casa a Nishioi) in early summer 2020

In terms of amounts of the many microorganisms that inhabit healthy soil, concrete- and asphalt-covered cities stand on weakened ground. But what happens if we minimize the sizes of building foundations and restore the surface layer of soil, and if we replace asphalt for motor vehicles with living, breathing soil inhabited by microorganisms? I believe that just such a vision of architecture and cities, framed in terms of soil ecology, is bound to emerge.

Human waste and food scraps, vital for soil microorganisms, must also be taken into account. Feces and urine flushed down toilets flow through sewer systems, are decomposed by microorganisms at sewage treatment plants, and are then disinfected with substances such as chlorine and discharged into the sea. Food waste is burned in incinerators and becomes ash. As food waste has high water content, incinerating it requires large quantities of energy. Clearly it is an important task to return some of this human waste and garbage to the soil, rather than simply treating it all as waste for disposal. To rethink the city literally from the ground up, it is first of all necessary for each dwelling to secure a supply of soil. This could enable human waste and garbage to decompose in small garden plots, and gardens to be connected by webs of mycelia, creating a nutrient and water network extending upward from the roots of plants.

Our *Holes In The House (Casa A Nishioi)* home/office had a small concrete-paved parking space, but lacking a car, we had no need for this. So, staff and interns worked together to strip away the concrete little by little and reveal the soil below. The quantity of fragmented concrete this produced was overwhelming, and what lay beneath was dead soil mixed with bits of crushed stone and mortar, containing no worms or pill bugs. Our first goal was to restore the soil to a healthy state, and we dug it up and turned it over to introduce fresh air. Then we dug a ditch at the edge of the garden, poured in bamboo charcoal powder, and laid crushed stone and dead branches on top of it to produce a water channel. Bamboo charcoal has a porous structure, and in addition to functioning as a deodorizer, has the effect of making it easier for water and air to penetrate the soil. We had been given oak and Japanese maple trees, which we planted after laying down bamboo charcoal and humus. Also, we made a homemade composter by blending peat moss and charcoal in a cardboard container, to which garbage such as vegetable scraps was added and aged for about two months, then mixed into the soil of the garden. We obtained some earthworms and let them loose in the soil, and about a year later, weeds grew and it became a living garden home to pill bugs, ants and crickets. Not only weeds such as dandelions and chickweed, but also pumpkin squashes, cherry tomatoes, and sweet potatoes grew from seeds buried in the compost. When the garden appears to be smothered by one type of weed, that weed withers and decomposes, and another kind of plant or flower flourishes. Vegetation in the garden changes drastically with each season, and they appear to be both competing and coexisting within the small territory of the garden. It is like a microcosm of life on Earth. With flowers, trees, small insects and invisible microbes living and breathing around us, we are learning more about life every day. Since the small parking space for a single car became a soil-filled garden, it feels many times larger and deeper than before.

Reference
– Hiroomi Takada, *The Soil Environment: Forgotten Perspectives on Symbiosis and Revival of Ancient Techniques*, Kenchiku Shiryo Kenkyusha, 2020.
– David R. Montgomery, Anne Bikle, *The Hidden Half of Nature: The Microbial Roots of Life and Health*, W. W. Norton & Company, 2016.

地球のための基礎

土壌から建築を考えてみると、土に接する部分である基礎が気になってくる。現在主流になっているのは鉄筋コンクリートのベタ基礎と布基礎である。コンクリートの基礎がなかった時代には基礎は石でつくられていた。民家園に行くと礎石や束石の上に柱が建てられ、地面に埋め込まれた石の上に土台が置かれている様子を見ることができる。雨の多く湿度の高い日本の多くの地域では、木材の腐食を防ぐために礎石と束によって床は地面から持ち上げられている。この考え方をもとに、石をコンクリートに置き換えたのが、在来工法の布基礎である。床下の湿気がこもらないように布基礎は地面から300mm以上立ち上がり、換気口が設けられる。この布基礎の形式は徐々にベタ基礎に変わっていく。ベタ基礎は、建物の重量を地盤全体に均等に伝えるため構造的にも都合がよい。さらにベタ基礎のコンクリートの下に気密フィルムを敷き込めば土からの湿気は室内に入り込まなくなり、床下の換気が不要になるため断熱もしやすい。家の床下は木材の腐食を防ぐための空間であり、ときには猫が雨風を凌ぐ場所だった。しかしベタ基礎の出現により、床下の無駄な空間は排除された。そのため土に対する想像力も失われてしまった。建築は大地に固定された存在である。大地との接続の仕方は本当にこれでいいのだろうか。

　ではもう一度、伝統構法に着目したらどうか。建築と大地との接点に厳しい気候風土との格闘と共存の跡が刻まれているはずである。伝統構法のなかでも石場建ては土壌中の通気と水脈を壊さない方法である。礎石が建物の重みで沈んでいかない

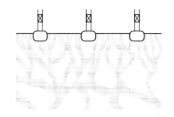

石場建ての基礎（左）と
コンクリートベタ基礎（右）
Raised stone foundation
(left) and flat concrete
foundation (right)

《明野の高床》模型（S=1/50）
1/50 scale model of *Akeno Raised-Floor House*

ように、礎石の下には細かい砂利が敷きつめられ、さらにその直下に焼いた松杭が打ち込まれている。炭化した松杭の多孔質表面には菌糸が張り巡りやすく、土壌と松杭を微生物の弱い力で一体化する。こうした伝統構法は現在の建築基準法で定められていない。法制度はコンクリートという材料を前提として組み立てられているようである。

　リサイクルができないコンクリートを使うのではなく、100%リサイクル可能な鉄で基礎をつくることを考えてみよう。鉄はもともと、酸化鉄という状態で地球上に存在する。地球の成分のなかで最も多いのが鉄の原子であるが、27億年前にシアノバクテリアと呼ばれる光合成能力を持った微生物が大量に発生したために、酸素濃度が上昇して海中の鉄イオンが酸素と結合して酸化鉄となり、海の底に堆積して鉄鉱床を形成した。鉄鉱石を高温にして酸素を取り除き、鉄が生産される。廃棄された鉄はチップ状になり再び溶解、圧延されて鋼材として再生する。

山梨県北杜市で計画している《明野の高床》では、土壌の微生物や水脈と共存する基礎の形式を考えている。そこでは伝統構法の松杭を現代の技術で応用して鋼管杭による高床形式の構造を提案した。土壌に接する部分は最小限となる。木造の建物本体は鋼管杭によって持ち上げられるため、地表面が覆われないため新鮮な水や空気が行き渡り、畑にも良い影響を与えるだろう。鋼管杭は軟弱な地盤の場合に杭の側面と地盤との摩擦に

鉄骨工場で製作された鉄板の独立基礎
Independent steel-plate foundation fabricated at steel-frame plant

よって荷重を支えるため頑丈な地盤では向いていない。現地で
地盤調査をしたところ支持層が浅いレベルにあるため、今回の
敷地では杭基礎は不向きであることがわかった。そこで杭では
なく、1.2m×1.2mの鉄板の底盤に十字に組んだ12mmの鉄板
を溶接した独立基礎によって建物を支える形式を採用した。土
を支持地盤近くまで掘り、約4mの間隔で合計10個の鉄の独立基
礎を設置する。その上に木造の軸組が載る。このような高床形
式の基礎は、土壌に新鮮な水や空気が行き渡るだけでなく、土
台や大引に使われる木材を乾燥状態にし、シロアリの被害を点
検することができる。

　建物を建てることは地球に負荷を与え、ゴミを増やし、土
壌を汚すことでもある。だが、基礎を根本的に見直せば建築は
土壌と共存できるはずだ。そのためにはコンクリートと所有権
と法制度の近代的な強固な繋がりを解き、土壌と基礎の新しい
繋がりを構築するべきだ。

参考文献
– 高田宏臣『土中環境——忘れられた共生のまなざし、蘇る古の技』（建築資料
　研究社、2020）

Foundations That Support the Earth

When thinking about architecture from the ground up, the mind naturally turns to the foundation, the part of a building in contact with the soil. In Japan today, the prevalent types are flat reinforced concrete foundations and a type known as *nunokiso* (lit. "fabric foundation," also called *renzoku kiso* or "continuous foundation," a type of direct footing that runs diagonally across corners and attaches to the building wall). In the days before concrete foundations, stone was used. Go to Nihon Minka-en (the Japan Open-Air Folk House Museum) and you can see pillars erected atop foundation stones and floor post footings, and foundations placed atop stones embedded in the ground. In many parts of Japan, a country with a rainy and humid climate, foundation stones and floor post footings are used to secure space between the floor and the ground and prevent wood from rotting. Based on this principle, conventional *nunokiso* replaces stones with concrete. A *nunokiso* is raised more than 300 millimeters above the ground and has ventilation openings to prevent moisture under the floor from being

鉄板の独立基礎の構造図
Structural drawing of independent steel-plate foundation

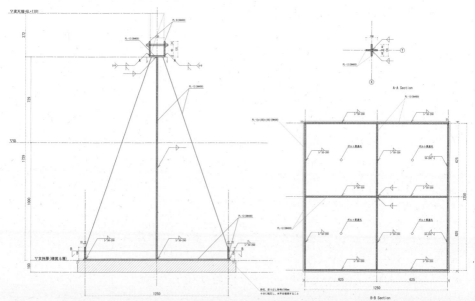

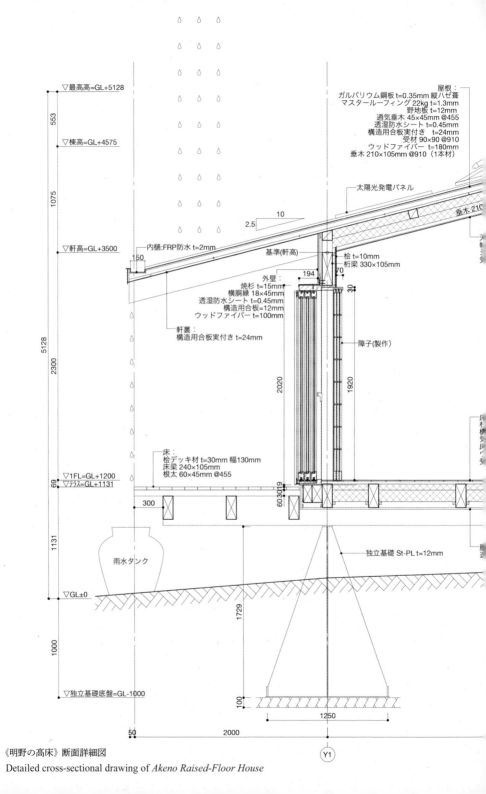

《明野の高床》断面詳細図

Detailed cross-sectional drawing of *Akeno Raised-Floor House*

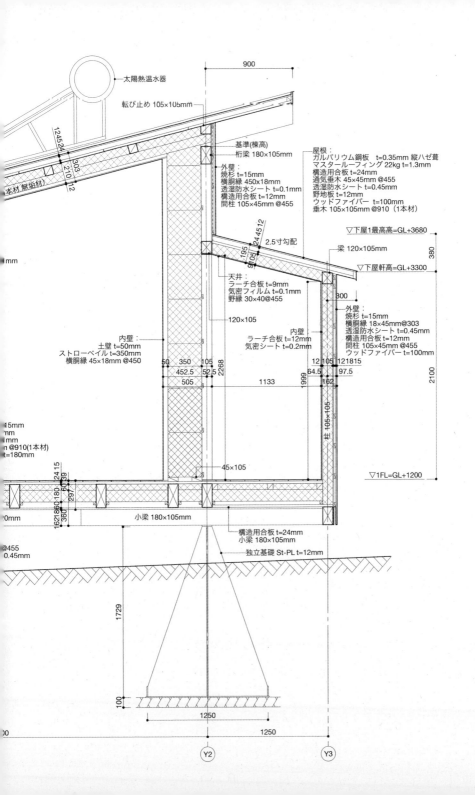

太陽熱温水器

転び止め 105×105mm

基準(棟高)
桁梁 180×105mm

外壁:
焼杉 t=15mm
横胴縁 450×18mm
透湿防水シート t=0.1mm
構造用合板 t=12mm
間柱 105×45mm @455

屋根:
ガルバリウム鋼板　t=0.35mm 縦ハゼ葺
マスタールーフィング 22kg t=1.3mm
構造用合板 t=24mm
通気垂木 45×45mm @455
透湿防水シート t=0.45mm
野地板 t=12mm
ウッドファイバー t=100mm
垂木 105×105mm @910（1本材）

2.5寸勾配

梁 120×105mm

▽下屋1最高高=GL+3680

▽下屋軒高=GL+3300

天井:
ラーチ合板 t=9mm
気密フィルム t=0.1mm
野縁 30×40@455

120×105

内壁:
ラーチ合板 t=12mm
気密シート t=0.2mm

内壁:
土壁 t=50mm
ストローベイル t=350mm
横胴縁 45×18mm @450

外壁:
焼杉 t=15mm
横胴縁 18×45mm@303
透湿防水シート t=0.45mm
構造用合板 t=12mm
間柱 105×45mm @455
ウッドファイバー t=100mm

柱 105×105

45×105

▽1FL=GL+1200

小梁 180×105mm

構造用合板 t=24mm
小梁 180×105mm

独立基礎 St-PL t=12mm

900

50　350　105
452.5　52.5
505

2268
1999

1133

12 105 121815
64.5　97.5
162

2100

380

300

1729

100

1250

1250

Y2　　Y3

敷地に設置された鉄板の独立基礎
Independent steel-plate foundation installed on-site

trapped. However, *nunokiso* have gradually given way to flat foundations, structurally convenient because they evenly distribute the weight of the building throughout the ground below. And if airtight film is laid under the concrete of a flat foundation, moisture from the soil will not enter the building, and ventilation under the floor will not be required, also making it easier to insulate. The crawlspaces under floors prevented wood from rotting, and sometimes cats sheltered there from the rain and wind. With the advent of flat foundations, however, this "wasted" space under the floor was eliminated. At the same time, we lost our mental picture of the soil below. A building is an immovable structure that sits on the Earth's surface. Is this really the right way to relate to the Earth?

Let us turn our attention once again to traditional construction methods. At points of contact between building and ground, there ought to be vestiges of both conflict and coexistence with the harsh climate and terrain. Among traditional approaches, stone construction is one that does not disrupt air flow and water veins in the soil. Fine gravel is laid under foundation stones so the stones do not sink under the weight of the building, and directly below the gravel are charred pine stakes are driven into the earth. Mycelia easily accumulate on the porous surface of the carbonized pine stakes, and soil and pine stakes are bound together by the subtle force of microorganisms. Such traditional construction methods are not regulated under the current Building Standards Law. The legal system too is apparently built on a foundation of concrete, with the supremacy of this material going unquestioned.

But what about the alternatives? Let us consider building foundations with 100% recyclable iron rather than non-recyclable concrete. Iron comes from the Earth, originally taking the form of iron oxide. In terms of number of atoms, iron is the most abundant component of the Earth, but approximately 2.7 billion years ago a large number of cyanobacteria (microorganisms capable of photosynthesis) were generated, causing oxygen levels to rise and iron ions in the oceans to bond with oxygen, which formed iron oxide that settled on the ocean floor as iron ore deposits. Today, it is by heating iron ore to high temperatures and removing the oxygen that we produce iron. Scrap iron can be crushed into chips, melted down, and rolled again to be reborn as steel.

For *Akeno Raised-Floor House*, a planned project in Hokuto, Yamanashi Prefecture, we considered types of foundations that coexist with the soil microorganisms and water veins below. We initially proposed a stilt structure utilizing steel pipe piles, using present-day technology to adapt the traditional pine-stake construction method. This would minimize the surface area of the structure in direct contact with the soil. With the main body of the wooden building raised on steel pipe piles, the ground's surface would remain uncovered, enabling fresh water and air to circulate and positively impacting farm fields as well. However, steel pipe piles support load through friction between the sides of the piles and the soil when driven into soft ground, and as such are not suitable for hard ground. A ground survey of the site revealed that a pile foundation was not appropriate for this site, as the hard, solid supporting layer of soil was not far below the surface. Thus the plan was modified, and in place of piles, the building is to be supported by independent foundation units consisting of 12mm iron-plate assembled in a cross formation and welded to the bottoms of 1.2 x 1.2-meter iron plates. The soil will be dug down to near the support layer, a total of 10 independent iron foundation units installed at intervals of approximately 4m, and a wood-frame structure placed on top of this. This raised-floor format will not only allow fresh water and air to penetrate the soil, but also dry the wood used for the house's base and sleepers (horizontal timbers near ground level), and enable inspection for termites.

Constructing buildings places a burden on the Earth, generates waste and pollutes the soil. However, if we fundamentally rethink foundations, buildings and the soil should be able to coexist harmoniously. To achieve this, the closely interconnected system of concrete, property ownership, and regulations in the modern era should be dismantled, and new relationships between soil and foundation established.

Reference
- Hiroomi Takada, *The Soil Environment: Forgotten Perspectives on Symbiosis and Revival of Ancient Techniques*, Kenchiku Shiryo Kenkyusha, 2020.

食べられない部分の建築

人間の生は植物の生と切り離せない。人類は呼吸し、植物の果実や種子や葉を食べ、木を煮炊きや暖を取る燃料とし、麻や綿などの植物で衣服をつくり、木や草を用いて住居をこしらえた。植物は太陽の光を受けて、二酸化炭素と水をブドウ糖に変え、それらが重合して複雑な有機物であるデンプンやセルロースがつくられる。デンプンを多く含む可食性のバイオマスである植物の種子や球根は炭水化物の貯蔵庫である。これが人間の主食となる。セルロースを多く含む非食性バイオマスである植物の幹や茎は、化学的に安定した強固な細胞組織の塊であり、資材や燃料として利用されてきた。

　植物のなかでも建材として使われているのは、主に樹木の幹の部分である。再生可能なマテリアルとして木材が注目されているが、木材以外の植物バイオマスにも建材としての可能性がある。例えば、それは稲、小麦、大麦等の穀物、茅、葦、ススキ、い草、竹などのイネ科の植物である。イネ科の植物の茎を乾燥させたものが藁である。藁は茅葺屋根、畳、小舞、土壁などの材料になる。人類は長い歴史のなかで身の回りの環境を食べ物に関連する植生へと変えた。藁葺屋根と土壁の民家をみると、農業の副産物を寄せ集めて生存環境をつくり出してきたことがわかる。

藁を材料にした家はストローベイルハウスと呼ばれている。麦藁や稲藁を圧縮したブロックを積み上げて藁壁の表面に粘土を塗り固めて家の壁になる。ストローベイルの壁の厚みは350〜450mm程度で、優れた断熱材にもなる。19世紀に藁を圧縮するベイラーという道具が発明され、樹木が育たない植生環境のアメリカにおいて藁が建設に応用されたのが始まりだそうである。現在はエコロジストたちによって化学合成物質を使わない材料として藁が注目され、建築家や研究者によって耐火性や耐水性、構法や構造に関する知見が蓄積されている。藁ブロックは

左：保管された藁ブロック
右：圧縮された麦藁
Left: Straw bales in storage
Right: Compressed wheat straw

　片手で持ち上げられる重さであることから、建設ワークショップが可能である。

　日本でもストローベイルハウス建設が各地で行われている。藁ブロックを積み、間柱の取り付けられた横胴縁にシュロ縄で括り付けて、竹串を上から刺して固定する。面積にもよるが、10人くらいで作業すれば2日間で藁積みは完了する。積み終わると、粘土と砂、藁を混ぜた団子状の荒土を手で藁ブロックに練りつけていく。日本では耐震性の観点からストローベイル自体を構造に用いることができないため、木造の柱梁の軸組構法と併用される。また日本の多雨で湿潤な気候では、土壁を雨や湿気から守るために庇を張り出し、基礎を高くしておく必要がある。湿気がこもると藁は発酵を始めてしまうからである。ストローベイルハウスは素人でも建設可能で、土に還る家である。私たちは《明野の高床》において、藁に湿気が溜まらないように、地面から浮いた高床形式にし、先人が培ってきたストローベイル構法の改良を試みている。

　竹も農業と建築に関わりのある材料である。竹は地下茎の節の部分の芽から新しい竹が生育する。竹の生育は非常に早く、1日で1mも伸びる場合もある。作物の収穫に使う籠、物干し竿、竹杭、竹垣、土壁の小舞など加工のしやすさからさまざまな用途の材料になる。フィリピンのマニラで竹を構造にした屋外劇

左：マニラ近郊での竹の収穫
右：基礎シリンダーに
埋め込まれた竹
Left: Harvesting bamboo
near Manila
Right: Bamboo embedded in
foundation cylinders

場を設計したことがある。モンスーン地域の気候における米食
との関連から建築をつくれないかと考えて、農業と建築を繋ぐ
材料として竹を選んだ。マニラ近郊の農家を訪れると、農家の
庭には株立ちの竹がたくさん生い茂っている。日本の竹とは異
なりフィリピンなどの赤道に近い地域の竹は肉厚で構造にも用
いることができる。農家では農機具や小屋などあらゆるものに
竹が使われている。その竹の風景から農業と建築は分離されて
おらず、一体的に結びついているように感じた。建築に竹を用
いるには工夫がいる。竹のなかは空洞であるため、木材のよう
にほぞ穴などの仕口や継手を加工することができない。竹の繊
維は筋状で割れやすいため、鉄の釘などの使用も好ましくない。
そのため縄や紐で縛ることで竹どうしを接合する。竹を構造に
用いるには害虫から保護することが大事になってくる。虫に食
べられる部分が弱くなるため、竹を伐採後すぐに根元からホウ
酸の溶液に浸し、毛細管現象を利用して竹全体に行き渡らせな
ければならない。木材は柱と梁の軸組に向いているが、竹は1
本の部材ではなく、複数の部材が群となり、その相互作用で構
造が成り立っている。竹は織物のような構法なのである。

農業の副産物で建築をつくることは、食べ物の食べられない部
分を使い尽くすことだ。自分の胃袋と自分の住まう環境が繋が
る。それは自分の内臓の世界と皮膚の外側の世界が一体的であ
ると感じさせてくれる。

122

Building With
the Inedible Parts

Human life is inseparable from plant life. Human beings breathe, eat the fruits, seeds and leaves of plants, use wood as fuel for cooking and heating, make clothing from plant fibers such as hemp and cotton, build dwellings with wood and grass. When plants absorb sunlight, they convert carbon dioxide and water into glucose, which polymerizes to produce complex organic substances such as starch and cellulose. Plants' seeds and bulbs, starch-rich edible biomass, are treasure chests of energy-giving carbohydrates, the staples of the human diet. Tree trunks and plant stalks, cellulose-rich inedible biomass, are sturdy, chemically stable cell tissue masses and have been used throughout history as building materials and fuel.

右：ナイロンで結ばれた竹の接合部
左：《Bamboo Theater》の竹フレーム
Left: Bamboo joints tied with nylon string
Right: Frame of *Bamboo Theater*

Of all vegetative matter, it is the trunks of trees that are most often used as building materials. Today wood is drawing new attention as a renewable material, but plant biomasses other than wood also have potential for use in building. Examples include grains such as rice, wheat and barley, and grasses such as reeds, rushes, pampas grass and bamboo. The stalks of grasses are dried to make various types of straw, which are used for thatched roofs, tatami mats, lath, and mud wall. Throughout our long history, humankind has transformed the environment around us into an agricultural one, putting food-related plants in place of others. When we see an old Japanese house with a thatched roof and a mud wall, it is evident that traditional living environments were created using various by-products of agriculture.

There are houses made with straw as a primary material, known as straw bale houses. Blocks of compressed wheat and rice straw are stacked and clay applied to their surface to form the walls of the house. The straw bales in these walls are about 350 to 450 millimeters thick, and they have excellent heat-insulating properties. In the 19th century, a straw-compressing implement known as a baler was invented and straw began to be used for construction in the United States, which has large treeless expanses. Today, ecologists are focusing on straw as a material that does not include chemically synthesized substances, and architects and researchers are amassing knowledge about its fire resistance, water resistance, construction methods and structure. Straw bales are light enough to lift with one hand, and construction workshops being are held in various locations.

Straw bale houses are being built in various locations in Japan as well. Straw bales are stacked, tied with hemp-palm rope to horizontal furring strips with studs mounted, and bamboo skewers are inserted from above to keep them in place. While the time required varies depending on the size of the house, a crew of 10 or so can finish stacking the straw in two days or so. After stacking is complete, round pieces of rough soil – a mixture of clay, sand, and straw – are kneaded into the straw bales by hand. In Japan, straw bales themselves cannot be used for the integral structure due to the need for seismic resistance, so they are used in conjunction with wood-frame column and beam construction. In Japan's rainy, humid climate, eaves must protrude and foundations must be raised to protect clay walls from rain and moisture, as straw begins to ferment when exposed to high humidity. A straw bale house can be built even by an amateur, and is biodegradable. In our *Akeno Raised-Floor House* project, we are endeavoring to improve on the straw bale construction methods developed by our predecessors, by separating the floor from the ground with a stilt-like structure so moisture does not accumulate in the straw.

Bamboo is another material that relates to both agriculture and architecture. New bamboo plants emerge from shoots, which are nodes of bamboo's underground rhizomes. Bamboo grows very quickly, sometimes as much as a meter a day. Because it is so easy to work with, it can be used for various purposes such as making baskets for harvesting crops, clothespins, stakes, fences, and the lath for wattle-and-daub walls. One of our past projects was a bamboo-frame open-air theater in Manila, the Philippines. Thinking about the relationship between the region's rice-based diet and monsoon climate,

左：《Bamboo Theater》
米袋の屋根葺き材
右：《Bamboo Theater》模型1/50
Left: Rice bags repurposed as roofing
material for *Bamboo Theater*
Right: 1/50 scale model of
Bamboo Theater

we selected bamboo as a material that connects agriculture and architecture. Upon visiting a farmhouse near Manila, we found its garden overgrown with bamboo. Unlike Japanese bamboo, bamboo in equatorial areas like the Philippines is thick and sturdy enough to be used for structural frameworks. On farms, bamboo is used to make everything from farming implements to sheds. Agriculture, architecture, and the bamboo-covered landscape seem inseparable, parts of a single whole. At the same time, there are certain tricks to building with bamboo. Because it is hollow inside, it is not possible to create joints and couplings with mortises as one would with wood. Bamboo fibers are striated and fragile, so iron nails and the like should not be used, and instead stalks of bamboo are joined by tying with rope or string. Also, using bamboo as a basic structural material requires protecting it from insects. Areas eaten by insects are weakened, and it is necessary to immerse entire bamboo plants in a boric acid solution down to the roots immediately after cutting them so the solution spreads throughout the bamboo via the capillary phenomenon. Wood timbers are geared toward frameworks of columns and beams, but with bamboo the basic unit is not a single stalk but an aggregate, and structural integrity is based on mutual interaction. Bamboo construction is a process like weaving fabric.

Building with agricultural by-products enables use of all the inedible parts of plants grown for food. Our stomachs and our living environments are connected. Seen in this light, the world of our internal organs and the world outside our skins seem like one.

木と火の行為可能性

陸上植物である樹木は、硬い細胞壁の成分であるセルロースとそれらを接着するリグニンという有機化合物によって構成されている。そのため樹木には重力や風にも対抗できるほどの強さがある。樹木の幹の内側の部分は死んだ細胞の束で、その外側の一部に生きている細胞がある。死んだ細胞は水を送る導管としての役割と骨のような構造としての役割がある。セルロースは強酸でも高熱でも細胞が壊れない強固な組織であるため、細胞が死んでも分解されにくい。樹木は死んだ細胞組織を利用して高く立ち、集合して森という巨大な環境を形成する。

左：製材所で削られた
丸太の皮
右：ストーブの燃料となる
ペレット
Left: Bark stripped off of
logs at a sawmill
Right: Wood pellets used
as fuel for stoves

建築史家レイナー・バンハムは『環境としての建築』のなかで、木材を利用する2つの基本的な方法に、「構造的な解決法」と「原動力で処理する解決法」があると述べている[1]。木の物質的で視覚的な側面ではなく、遊牧民の暮らしのように焚き火を囲んだ熱・光のエネルギーに着目した建築論である。最近注目される木材のカスケード利用は物質とエネルギーの両面を繋ぐ方法である。分厚く、太く、長い材料を使って大規模木造建築をつくり、そこで廃棄される木材を小さな建築に使い、またそこで廃

棄される木材を家具の材料にし、最終的に粉々にして燃料にする。木材の持つ物質としての可能性を最大限利用し、最後にエネルギーとして使い切ろうとする考え方である。

　《西大井のあな》に暖を取るためにペレットストーブを導入した。ペレットが炎を上げて燃え尽きていく様子を見ていると心地よさを感じる。ペレットは木材製材所で発生する丸太の樹皮、大鋸屑、端材などの工場残材が圧縮されて製造される。いわば屑や滓である。タンクからペレットがポロポロとストーブのなかに落ちて、炎が持続する。ストーブの鋳物の天板は着火してから1時間でおよそ200度の高温になる。この熱がもったいないためホーロー鍋で煮込み料理をしたり、サツマイモをアルミホイルで包んで焼き芋をすることが増えた。《西大井のあな》には、1階天井から4階床まで穴が開いているためストーブを点けると上階では室温が2〜5度程度上昇する。ひと繋がりの空間では重力によって暖気は上へ、冷気は下へ移動し、熱の不均質状態ができる。こうした不均質さを利用するために4階で洗濯物を干している。窓を開ければ重力換気ができるため物干しには最適である。夏は2階のひんやりしたゲストルームに避難して寝る。この熱的不均質状態を空調によって解消するのではなく、むしろ不均質さに合わせて人間のほうが快適な場所を選んでいくことで、熱エネルギーを使い切っている。

　樹木の細胞の死骸の塊は太陽のエネルギーを浴びて水を吸い上げて生きてきた痕跡である。それが火となってエネルギーを生み出す。こうした木の行為可能性が尽くされていくことに心地よさを感じる[2]。それは生きているものが成長する喜びと似ている。建物をつくるときにも使うときにも、可能性を尽くす感覚が生態学的なデザインの基盤となるだろう。

参考文献

1——レイナー・バンハム『環境としての建築——建築デザインと環境技術』(堀江悟郎訳、SD選書、2013／原著＝1969)

2——柳澤田実「可能性を尽くす楽しみ、可能性が広がる喜び——倫理としての生態学」(村田純一ほか編『知の生態学的転回 第3巻 倫理 人類のアフォーダンス』東京大学出版、2013)

Behavioral Potential of Wood and Fire

Trees – plants that grow on land – are comprised of cellulose, which makes up their hard cell walls, and an organic compound called lignin, which acts like an adhesive to bind the cell walls together. This makes trees strong enough to withstand gravity and wind. The interior of a tree trunk is a bundle of dead cells, with some living cells among those on its periphery. Dead cells serve as conduits for water, and form a skeleton-like structure. Cellulose is such a sturdy tissue that cell walls do not break even when exposed to strong acid or high heat, and tend not to decompose even if cells die. Trees use their dead cell tissue to grow to great heights, and gathered together, they form the vast biosphere we call a forest.

The architectural historian Reyner Banham states in *Architecture of the Well-Tempered Environment*[1] that there are two basic methods of using wood: the "structural solution" and the "power-operated solution," i.e. using wood to build a structure or to generate energy. Banham points out that thus far, architects and historians have focused only on the material and visual aspects of wood, and failed to examine it as a source of heat and light energy, as when nomadic people gather around bonfires. His is an architectural theory that focuses on energy rather than matter. One method of connecting the material and energy aspects, which has been attracting attention recently, is known as cascading use of wood. Long, thick, heavy timbers are used to construct large-scale wooden buildings, the wood discarded from these projects is used for smaller buildings, the wood

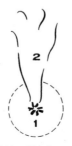

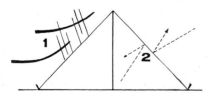

天幕の環境的行動。
1　天幕は風を避け雨をしめ出す。
2　大部分の輻射を反射し、内部の熱を保持し、日射熱を排除し、プライバシーを維持する。

焚火のまわりの環境条件。
1　輻射熱および光の帯域。
2　温気および煙の風下へのたなびき。

引用出典＝レイナー・バンハム『環境としての建築──建築デザインと環境技術』(SD選書、2013)
Source of quotes: Reyner Banham, *Architecture of the Well-Tempered Environment* (SD Sensho, 2013)

ペレットストーブの炎
Fire in a pellet stove

discarded from these is used in turn to make furniture, and finally the leftovers are pulverized for use as fuel. The idea is to maximize the potential of wood as a material, and finally use it up as energy.

Our *Holes In The House (Casa A Nishioi)* project incorporates a pellet stove for heating. It is pleasing to see the pellets burn, eventually incinerated to nothing. Wood pellets used as fuel for stoves are manufactured by compressing factory residue such as bark, sawdust, and scraps from sawmills, what could be described as waste or dregs. Pellets trickle down into the stove from a tank behind it, fueling the fire and enabling the stove to keep burning. The stove's cast-iron top reaches a peak temperature of about 200 degrees Celsius an hour after it is lit, and it is becoming more common for people to cook in an enameled metal pot, or wrap sweet potatoes in aluminum foil and place them on the top to roast, rather than letting this heat go to waste. At *Holes In The House (Casa A Nishioi)* there is an opening extending from the ceiling of the first floor to the floor of the fourth. When the stove is lit, the room temperature on the upper floors rises approximately two to five degrees. In a connected space, warm air rises and cold air sinks, as gravity causes uneven distribution of heat. Laundry is hung to dry on the fourth floor to take advantage of this uneven distribution, and the space is ideal for this task as opening the windows creates buoyancy-based ventilation. In summer occupants move to the cooler guest room on the second floor. Instead of using air conditioning to eliminate uneven heat distribution, thermal energy is fully utilized by having multiple options from which people choose the most comfortable location.

Wood scraps are converted to thermal energy, warming people and heating food. People move around in response to warm air's natural tendency, which is to rise. Wood is a mass of dead tree cells, but having been exposed to the sun's energy and absorbing water, it retains vestiges of when it was alive. It becomes fire and produces energy. It is pleasant to see all the behavioral potential of wood being exhausted,[2] something like the joy of seeing a living thing grow. Moving forward, whether building with wood or using it, the sense that we have utilized its full potential will be the basis of ecological design.

References
1——Reyner Banham, *Architecture of the Well-Tempered Environment* (translated by Goro Horie, SD Sensho, 2013. Originally published 1969).
2——Tami Yanagisawa, "The Joy of Utilizing All Possibilities, the Thrill of Seeing Possibilities Expand: Ecology as Ethics," in Junichi Murata et al. eds., *The Ecological Turn: New Philosophical and Psychological Perspectives on Human Studies, Vol. 3 – Ethics and Ecology of the Social Environment*, University of Tokyo Press, 2013.

オフグリッドシステムと
生活の主体性

日本各地でメガソーラー建設計画がある。多いところで10万枚
以上のパネルが敷き詰められる。メガソーラーは次世代の再生可
能エネルギーの大規模事業である。メガソーラーによる発電は、
放射能汚染が懸念される原子力発電やCO_2を大量に排出する火
力発電よりずっと好ましいと思っていた。しかしメガソーラー
事業の実情は、大規模に地形を改変し、巨大な山林を削り、土
壌、水脈、生態系を根こそぎに破壊することだった。発電パネル
を設置するためには平坦な場所が必要で、雑草が生えないよう
に除草剤を撒き、砕石を敷き詰め、架台を建てるそうだ。地形
や生態系を破壊したならば水害や土砂崩れが起きやすい危険な
状態になる。このような事業が推進される背景には、地方自治
体の財政が困窮するなか、国の補助金などを利用した大規模事

左：サトウさんのオフグリッドハウス。8枚のパネルで発電
右：サトウさんのオフグリッドハウス夜景。昼間に蓄えられた電力で灯された光
Left: Ms. Sato's off-grid house. Power is generated with eight solar panels
Right: Night view of Ms. Sato's off-grid house. Lights are powered with
electricity stored during the day

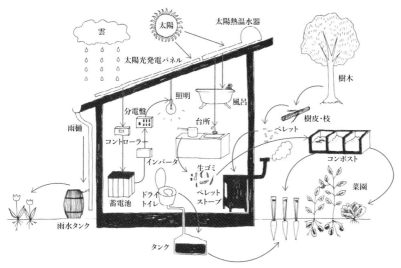

オフグリッドハウスの仕組み
Functional diagram of an off-grid house

業によって新たな雇用の創出が見込めることが挙げられる。地球環境問題が権力のなかに取り込まれる構造になっている。これからますます、ジオガバナンス（地球統治）の暴走が、あらゆるところで引き起こされることが懸念される。メガソーラーに反対する人が「メガソーラーは怖い、でも家についているソーラーパネルはまだ可愛らしい」と言っていた。ソーラーパネルそのものに罪はない（パネルの製造とリサイクルの問題は残されているとしても）。人間を超えた巨大なスケールを生み出してしまうことに問題の本質がある。この「可愛らしい」という言葉は規模の問題を言い当てている。巨大なものへの怖さと脆弱さ。それが露呈したのは福島原発事故ではなかったか。この巨大な中心構造を是正するべきである。建物にエネルギーの分散と自律性が求められる。

　こうしたエネルギーの自律性を実現する「オフグリッドハウス」という住宅の仕組みがある。いわば住宅が極小発電所なのだ。オフグリッドとは電力網（グリッド）に繋がれていない（オフ）という意味である。東日本大震災を契機に自分たちで電力をつくりたいという人が増えている。オフグリッドハウスに暮らす人たちは太陽とともに人間が生きていることを深く実感しており、太陽を取り入れたさまざまな暮らしの工夫を実践して

いる。例えば、電気冷蔵庫を持たず、夏は日陰となる冷涼室に野菜を保存し、冬には外気を利用した天然冷蔵庫を使う。曇りや雨の日が続き充電が少ないときには薪コンロを使用するため煮込み料理を楽しむ。太陽の熱を集めて給湯に使う場合、晴れた日はお湯が大量にできるので、家族みんなでお風呂を楽しむ。そうした太陽のリズムと連動した暮らしをしていると、不思議なことに健康になるそうである。そして「電力を買わないことで清々しい気持ちになった」と皆、口を揃えて言う。発電と充電の技術によって、自然とともに暮らすという生活様式が現れてきている。

　私たちの生活は冷蔵庫、電子レンジ、エアコン、洗濯機などの家電製品によって成り立っている。これらの家電製品は発電所から無限に電力が供給されることを前提に製造され、私たちの暮らしに入り込んでいる。それに対してオフグリッドシステムでの電力エネルギーは有限である。太陽が沈み、雨や曇りの日が続けば発電できず、充電されたエネルギーがなくなれば電気は使えなくなる。オフグリッドシステムという技術体系は、家電製品が属している技術体系とは対立している。エネルギーが無限か有限かで技術を捉える思想が異なるのである。こうした異なる系の技術がオフグリッドハウスでは共存しており、生活する人は自分で考えて家電製品の使用を制限したり、使い方を工夫したり、そもそも家電製品を購入しないなど、さまざまな可能性に開かれていくのである。それは自分の生活を主体的に創造していくことに繋がっている。このように技術によって私たちの主体性は媒介されているのである。太陽エネルギーを貯めて使うというエネルギーの有限性によって、生活と技術の間に参加の関係が築かれているのだ。

参考文献
－ サトウチカ『ひらけ！オフグリッド──電線切ったら、楽しい暮らしが待っていた』（フォレスト出版、2019）
－ フジイチカコ『ソーラー女子は電気代0円で生活してます！』（KADOKAWA、2017）
－ ピーター＝ポール・フェルベーク『技術の道徳化──事物の道徳性を理解し設計する』（鈴木俊洋訳、法政大学出版局、2015／原著＝2011）

Off-Grid Systems and Autonomous Lifestyles

There are plans for construction of mega solar power plants in various parts of Japan, many of which call for laying 100,000 or more panels side by side. Mega solar has become a major sector of the next-generation renewable energy industry. I formerly believed that mega solar was much preferable to nuclear power, due to concerns about radioactive contamination, and to fossil-fuel power generation, which emits massive amounts of CO_2. However, in practice mega solar facilities necessitate large-scale modification of the terrain, massive deforestation of mountainous areas, and wholesale destruction of soil, groundwater, and ecosystems. Installation of solar panels requires flat land, on which herbicides are spread to prevent weeds from growing, gravel laid, and frameworks erected. If the terrain and ecosystem are devastated, it will lead to dangerous conditions under which floods and landslides are likely to occur. Underlying the advancement of such projects are the dire financial straits in which many local governments find themselves, and the fact that such massive national government-subsidized projects can be expected to create jobs. The system is such that the interests of those in power override global environmental concerns, and there are concerns in every region that geo-governance will spiral out of control in the coming years. One opponent of mega solar has said that "mega solar is frightening, but solar panels mounted on the roofs of houses are still charming." Solar panels themselves are innocent (even if there are persistent problems with their manufacturing and recycling): the essence of the problem here is the construction of colossal structures that transcend human scale. The mega solar critic's word "charming" speaks to this issue of scale. Colossal structures are both frightening and fragile – wasn't this the lesson we learned from the Fukushima nuclear power plant disaster? We need to shift away from the paradigm of enormous, centralized structures. What we need instead are buildings with diversified and autonomous energy sources.

An "off-grid house" is a housing system that achieves this energy autonomy. A house of this type can be described as a micro-power plant. "Off-grid" means not connected to the electrical power network, and the number of people who want to generate their own electricity has increased since the Great East Japan Earthquake of 2011. Occupants of off-grid houses are deeply and keenly aware of humanity's coexistence with the sun, and incorporate it into various lifestyle practices. For example, they may live without an electric refrigerator, storing vegetables in a cool, shaded room in the summer and using the outdoors as a natural fridge in the winter. When it is cloudy or rainy and solar power is running low they use a wood-burning stove, on which they prepare stewed dishes. When the sun's heat is collected and used for hot water supply, large amounts of hot water can be produced on sunny days, so the whole family can enjoy bathing. Off-grid house dwellers say that living in sync with the sun's rhythms has astounding health benefits, and all agree that they feel invigorated by not purchasing electricity. As power generation and storage technologies advance, new lifestyles in harmony with nature are emerging.

Our contemporary lifestyles are wholly dependent on household appliances such as refrigerators, microwaves, air conditioners and washing machines. These appliances, manufactured on the premise that power plants will supply electricity indefinitely, have infiltrated every corner of our lives. Meanwhile, electrical power in off-grid systems is finite. When the sun goes down or there is a string of rainy or cloudy days, electricity cannot be generated, and if stored energy is exhausted, electricity cannot be used. Off-grid systems are a technological framework that opposes the framework to which household appliances belong. One's mentality toward technology differs depending on whether energy is perceived as infinite or as finite. Technologies from these competing frameworks coexist in the off-grid house, and all sorts of possibilities emerge as people who live in these houses think of their own ways of limiting household appliance use, devising efficient means of using them or not buying them in the first place. This leads to independent creation of autonomous lifestyles, illustrating how our autonomy is facilitated and mediated by technologies. The finite nature of energy when solar energy is stored and used creates participatory relationships in the zone between technology and lifestyle.

References
  – Sato Chika, *Open! Off-Grid: Cut the Cable and Discover Joyful Living*, Forest Publishing, 2019.
  – Fujii Chikako, *Solar Women Live with Zero Electricity Bills!*, Kadokawa, 2017.
  – Peter-Paul Verbeek, *Moralizing Technology: Understanding and Designing the Morality of Things* (translated by Suzuki Toshihiro, Hosei University Press, 2015; original book published 2011).

太陽と調理

ソーラークッキングとは、太陽のエネルギーを利用した燃料不要の調理方法のことである。私は主に「エコ作」と呼ばれる調理器を利用している。ガラスの真空二重管のなかに巻きついた黒い金属膜が熱を吸収し、魔法瓶のようなガラス管内には熱が蓄積され200度程度に達する。ガラス管内に、角切りにしたトマト、ナス、パプリカ、玉ねぎ、そして塩を少々入れ、晴天時に30〜40分程度、太陽のほうへ向けて置いておく。水を使わなくても野菜から水分が出てジューシーなラタトゥイユが完成する。ガラス管に入るサイズに切ったりんご、レーズン、シナモンを入れて30分放置すれば、レーズンが少し焦げて香ばしいアップルシナモンができる。イベントではクッキーや餃子にも挑戦した。ソーラークッキングの調理器には主に4種類あり、1つ目はパラボラ形状の反射板で1カ所に集光する方法。2つ目は平滑な反射板を使って鍋などの調理器具に光を当てて加熱する方法で、ダンボールなどで簡単に製作できDIY向きである。3つ目はソーラーオーブンといわれるもので、断熱された箱に集光して加熱する方法。4つ目はチューブ状のガラスの真空管を利用する方法。このほかにも、太陽の熱を蒸気に変換したり、蓄熱して夜でも調理ができるようにする技術も開発されているようである。

　人間の食に独自なのは火、水、油を使って調理することである。一般的な家庭ではガスコンロ、IHヒーター、オーブン、電子レンジなどの調理機器はキッチンに格納されている。調理のための熱源はガスか電気である。ガスは石油コンビナートを経由し、油田へと繋がり、電気は電力網を通じて発電所と繋がっている。このようなインフラが整備されることで人間の食は成立している。しかしソーラークッキングは、太陽のエネルギーを利用するため、屋上や窓辺、屋外空間が調理の舞台となり、食材はキッチンから脱出して太陽のほうへ向かう。ソーラークッキングはどうやら洗濯物に近い存在だ。この無料の太陽エネルギーをもっと利用しようとするならば、ソーラークッキングは、

左：移動可能なソーラークッキングカート
右：真空ガラス二重管に食材を入れる
Left: A movable solar cooking cart
Right: Placing ingredients in double glass
vacuum tubes

キッチンそのもののあり方を変容させ、家のプランニング、生活の仕方までもが変容するかもしれないと想像させてくれる。

　ソーラークッキングをさらに発展させて移動式のソーラークッキングカートを制作した。このカートには8本の「エコ作」が搭載でき、まな板、包丁、皿、食材などが収納でき、車輪がついている。太陽高度の低い冬にも対応できる45度の角度に「エコ作」がセットできるようにした。車輪があるので簡単に太陽の方向に調理器具を向けることができる。スマホのアプリを利用すれば、都市のちょっとした隙間でも何時から何時まで太陽が出てくるか事前に調べることができ、調理時間などの予定を立てられる。東京では冬のほうが晴天率が高いため、冬のソーラークッキングも十分に可能だ。太陽が当たるところであれば、都市の隙間、広場、公園で料理ができ、インフラに繋がれていないからこそ、都市のパブリッククッキングができる。

　学生向けのワークショップでは、ソーラークッキングの調理器から製作することに挑戦した。材料はダンボール、アルミホイル、ミラーシール、アクリル板などで、手軽につくることができる。ある学生チームは放物線を計算し、直径1.8mの巨大

なパラボラ型の集光器を製作した。パラボラの中心にフライパンを設置し、ステーキを1時間かけて焼き上げた。別のチームはダンボールとミラーシールでつくったソーラーオーブンのなかに丸い鉄板を設置して、手作りピザを焼いた。私たちは雲間から太陽が現れると喜び、雲に隠れると落ち込んだ。もしかしたら太古の人々はこのように太陽に接していたのではないかと想像した。

　このようにソーラークッキングの面白いところは、インフラという強い繋がりを切り離し、太陽という資源に繋ぎ直すところである。こうした調理という日常の行為から、私たちが生きている社会を見直し、行きすぎた繋がりを緩めることができる。そしてまろやかな味とともに、太陽の恵みに触れることができるのである。

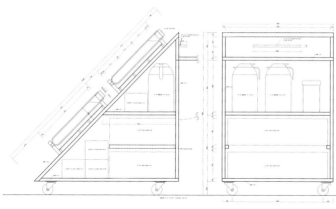

上：ソーラークッキングカートの図面
下：ソーラークッキングの調理器具の種類
Above: Drawing of solar cooking cart
Bottom: Types of cooking utensils for solar cooking

	パラボラ型	パネル型	ボックス型	真空管型
原理	放物線形の反射柜により1点に集光	反射板により集光	箱内部に集熱	管内部に集熱
利点	短時間で高温に達する	簡単で安価に製作可能	保温可能	高温に達する
欠点	頻繁に反射板の角度調整が必要	高温になりにくい	高温になりにくい	ガラス管が割れやすい

The Sun and Cooking

Solar cooking is fuel-free cooking using energy from the sun. Personally, I primarily use a cooking utensil called an Eco-saku for solar cooking. In an Eco-saku, black metal film wrapped around the inside of a double glass vacuum tube absorbs heat, and heat accumulates in the tube like inside a thermos, reaching approximately 200 degrees Celsius. You can prepare a juicy ratatouille without boiling water by putting diced tomato, eggplant, bell pepper, onion, and a little salt in the glass tube and leave it facing the sun for about 30 to 40 minutes in fine weather, which causes the vegetables to cook in their own evaporating moisture. Or, make a fragrant apple-cinnamon dessert by cutting apples, raisins, and cinnamon to a size that fits in the glass tube and leaving it for 30 minutes so the raisins become slightly charred. At events, we have also tried our hand at making cookies and gyoza dumplings.

There are four main types of solar cooking procedures. One is using a parabola-shaped reflector to concentrate sunlight in one spot. The second is using a smooth reflector to shine light on a cook-

屋上でソーラークッキングワークショップ
Solar cooking workshop on the rooftop

左：ソーラークッカーで
焼いたピザ・マルゲリータ
右：オートミールクッキー
Left: Pizza Margherita
baked in a solar cooker
Right: Oatmeal cookies

ing utensil such as a pot and heat it up. This reflector can easily be made with cardboard or other materials, and is DIY-friendly. The third employs a solar oven, which concentrates sunlight to generate heat inside an insulated box, and the fourth is the glass vacuum-tube method. In addition to these, technologies that convert the sun's heat into steam, or store heat so that cooking can be done even at night, have apparently been developed.

Cooking with fire, water, and oil is a practice unique to the human diet. In a typical household, cooking equipment such as gas ranges, induction heating cookers, ovens, and microwaves are kept in the kitchen, and the sources of heat for cooking are gas or electricity. Gas comes to us from oil fields via petrochemical complexes, and electricity from power plants via the grid. The modern human diet depends on having this infrastructure in place. Meanwhile, solar cooking uses the sun's energy and is done on rooftops, windowsills, or outdoor spaces, releasing ingredients from the kitchen and exposing them the sun. Solar cooking somehow resembles doing laundry. For those who endeavor to make greater use of this free solar energy, solar cooking can transform the kitchen itself, and one can imagine it transforming the way we plan our homes and even our ways of life.

We created a mobile solar cooking cart as a further development of solar cooking. This wheeled cart can accommodate eight Eco-saku units, and can store cutting boards, knives, plates and ingredients. The Eco-saku units can be set at a 45-degree angle to be used even in winter when the sun is low, and the wheels make it easy to point cookware in the direction of the sun. With a smartphone app, it is possible to check from what time to what time the sun will shine even in a small urban niche, and schedule cooking times and so forth. In Tokyo, the probability of clear skies is higher in winter, so solar cooking is also feasible during this season. One can cook in small interstices, plazas, and parks in the city, anywhere the sun shines, and because there is no need to connect to infrastructure, urban public cooking can be achieved.

At a workshop for students, we attempted solar cooking beginning with fabrication of cooking utensils. These can easily be made from such materials as cardboard, aluminum foil, mirrored sticker sheets, and acrylic panels. One team of students calculated the curve of a parabola and created a huge parabolic concentrator with a diameter of 1.8 meters. A frying pan was placed in the center of the parabola, and a steak was cooked in one hour. Another team placed a round iron plate in a solar oven made of cardboard and mirror sticker sheets, and baked homemade pizza. We all felt elated when the sun came out from behind a cloud, and crestfallen when it hid behind a cloud once more. One could imagine that people in ancient times related to the sun in a similar way.

The fascinating thing about solar cooking is that it releases us from our dependence on infrastructure and reconnects us to the sun as a resource. Through the seemingly mundane daily activity of cooking, we can re-examine the society in which we live and loosen our excessive connectedness. And we can enjoy the blessings of the sun, along with the delightfully mellow flavors of solar-cooked food.

BOILED CHICKEN TOMATO

ecosaku recipe

鶏もも肉　　とまと1個　　玉ねぎ1個

ブロッコリー　　にんにく1かけ

調味料：塩・コンソメ・醤油・ケチャップ

①鶏もも肉とトマト・玉ねぎ・ブロッコリーを食べやすい大きさに切る。
ニンニクは薄切りしておく。②①で切った材料に塩・コンソメ・醤油・ケ
チャップを入れ混ぜる。③工作に詰め、日光の当たる場所に1時間程度
おく。④肉に火が通っていることを確認し、お皿に盛り付けたら完成。

1/11 (水) 5℃ 11:00〜12:00

ソーラークッキングレシピ
A solar cooking recipe

141

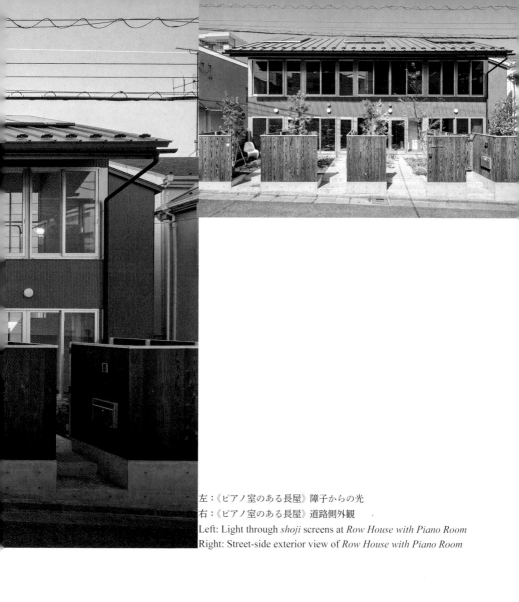

左：《ピアノ室のある長屋》障子からの光
右：《ピアノ室のある長屋》道路側外観
Left: Light through *shoji* screens at *Row House with Piano Room*
Right: Street-side exterior view of *Row House with Piano Room*

エレメントの生態学的複合

屋根や窓の慣習性について指摘した建築家ロバート・ヴェンチューリは「慣習的な部分を慣習にはずれて組み合わせることによって、新しい意味を産み出すことも可能である」と述べた[1]。ヴェンチューリの住宅作品では窓が屋根に割り込んでお互いが歪みながら絡み合っており、屋根と窓という慣習的なエレメントの持つ文脈を用いながらも、非慣習的な仕方で統合されていると読み取ることができる。こうした建築の部分と全体の関係はしばしば言語に喩えられる。建築の柱や床や窓などのさまざまな要素は「単語」に、それらの構成法は「文法」と捉えることができる。ヴェンチューリの建築のレトリックは人間の言語的な認識の枠組みを利用したものである。ヴェンチューリが活躍した同時代、1973年に起きたオイルショックを契機に、アメリカでは「ソーラーハウス」や「オートノマスハウス」など石油資源や火力発電に頼らずに太陽エネルギーを最大限活用する住宅が建設されている[2]。ソーラーハウスでは、最大限開けられた窓が南に向けられ、窓の内側には蓄熱壁がある。オートノマスハウスでは南に傾斜する屋根勾配の上に発電パネルが積載されている。これらの住宅では太陽エネルギーを得るために屋根や窓が自然の事物の摂理に従って配置されている。これらの住宅には2つの極端な傾向が指摘できる。一方は屋根や窓というエレメントを「意味」として扱っており、他方はそれらを「事物」として扱っていることである。

　こうしたヴェンチューリの複合のあり方を意味の問題だけに限定するのではなく、私はむしろ生態学的な事物の繋がりへと広げてみたいと思う。建築の諸要素が持ちつ持たれつの相互的関係において存在するよう、組織化するのである。

《ピアノ室のある長屋》(2019) は、住宅地に立地するピアノ教室付きの住宅とSOHO型の賃貸住戸が複合した長屋である。グランドピアノ2台が設置されているピアノ教室には地域の子ども

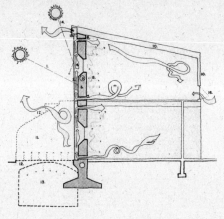

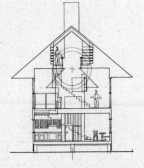

左：ロバート・ヴェンチューリ《Tucker House》(1975)
引用出典＝『a + u』1978年1月号（エー・アンド・ユー）
右：ダグラス・ケルボウ《Kelbaugh House》(1975)
Left: Robert Venturi, *Tucker House* (1975)
Source of quotes: *a+u*, January 1978.
Right: Douglas Kelbaugh, *Kelbaugh House* (1975)

や大人が訪れる。これらは住宅でありながら、その一部が地域に開放されるため、道路側にピアノ教室の待合室と玄関土間が集約され、アルミサッシの窓が連続した構えになっている。窓の奥に連なる明かり障子は、開閉によって視線を調整すると同時に、冷気や暖気を吹き抜け部分に逃がさない工夫である。約30度に傾けられた土間の屋根には太陽熱給湯のパネルが設置され、集められた熱は貯湯タンク内を経由して給湯や床暖房に利用される。鉄筋コンクリート造は木造と比べて、高コストで、製造過程においてCO_2排出量が多く、リサイクルが難しいことから、当初はすべて木造とする計画であった。しかし敷地背後に3mの高さを超える崖があり、条例により崖先端から30度ラインより下方に崖崩れから守る防護壁が求められるため、鉄筋コンクリート造の箱に木造の覆いが被さる構成とした。さらにコンクリートを構造的な役割だけでなく、熱環境や音環境を向上させる要素へ捉え直した。具体的には、コンクリートの蓄熱材料としての性質を生かして、冬の日射や床暖房の熱がコンクリートの躯体に蓄積されるようにし、コンクリートの重量を活かしてピアノ室の防音の効果を高めている。ピアノ室の仕上げにはフラッターエコー防止のための杉下見板、吸音のためのグラス

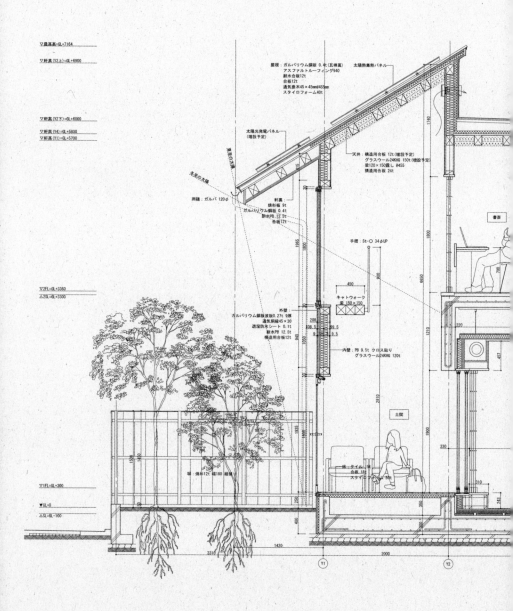

《ピアノ室のある長屋》断面詳細図

Detailed cross-sectional drawing of *Row House with Piano Room*

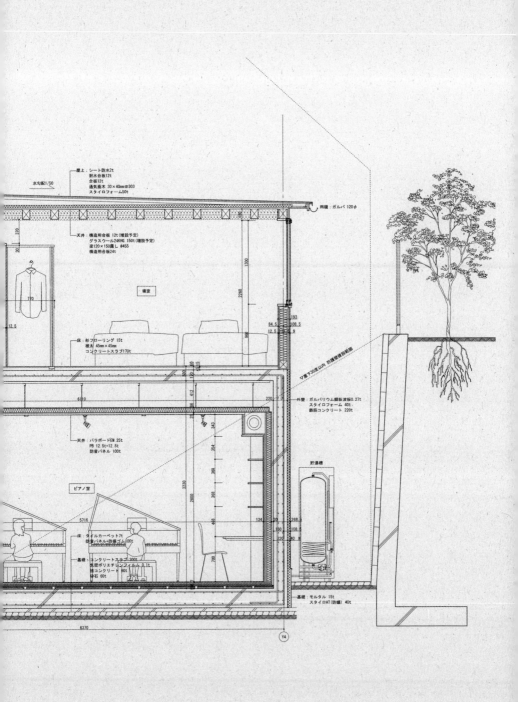

水勾配1/50

屋上：シート防水2t
　　　耐水合板12t
　　　合板12t
　　　通気胴木 30×40mm@303
　　　スタイロフォーム50t

雨樋：ガルバ 120φ

天井：構造用合板 12t（増設予定）
　　　グラスウール2400HG 150t（増設予定）
　　　梁120×150置し #455
　　　構造用合板24t

寝室

床：杉フローリング 15t
　　根太 45mm×45mm
　　コンクリートスラブ170t

▽庭下30度以内 防護範囲設定範囲

外壁：ガルバリウム鋼板波板0.27t
　　　スタイロフォーム 40t
　　　鉄筋コンクリート 220t

天井：パラボードEM 25t
　　　PB 12.5t+12.5t
　　　防音パネル 100t

貯湯槽

ピアノ室

床：タイルカーペット7t
　　防音パネル+防振ゴム 100t

基礎：コンクリートスラブ 300t
　　　精密ポリエチレンフィルム 0.1t
　　　捨コンクリート 60t
　　　砕石 60t

基礎：モルタル 15t
　　　スタイロAT（防蟻）40t

Y4

左：《ピアノ室のある長屋》待合室の土間
右：《ピアノ室のある長屋》ピアノ室
Left: Tile-floored waiting room at *Row House with Piano Room*
Right: Piano room at *Row House with Piano Room*

ウールボードとカーペットを用いた。コンクリートの打ち放し仕上げは硬質で冷たい印象であるため、障子紙や杉材、麻とパルプが編み込まれた壁紙などの柔らかで肌理細かい素材が並存することにより、複合的な知覚が呼び起こされるようにした。このようにコンクリートは、崖崩れからの防護、太陽光や熱の利用、ピアノの防音という複合的な役割を担っている。また土間の窓と障子の連なり、30度に傾けられた屋根、雨樋から集められた雨水と前庭の植栽の水やりなどが相互に関係し合っている。太陽・雨・崖・植物・音といった事物が、屋根・窓・障子・コンクリート壁といった諸要素によって生態学的に組織化されている。これがエレメントの生態学的複合の一例である。

参考文献
1——R・ヴェンチューリ『建築の多様性と対立性』（伊藤公文訳、鹿島出版会、1982）／原著＝1966）
2——Giovanna Borasi, Mirko Zardini, *Sorry, Out of Gas: Architecture's Response to the 1973 Oil Crisis* (Canadian Center for Architecture, 2007).

An Ecosystemic Composite of Elements

The architect Robert Venturi noted the conventionality of roofs and windows in architectural design, and wrote that "through unconventional organization of conventional parts [the archiect] is able to create new meanings within the whole." [1] In Venturi's residential works, windows intersect with roofs and both are reshaped and intertwined, in what can be seen as an example of unconventional combination that nonetheless retains the context of the conventional elements of roof and window. Such relationships between parts and whole in architecture is often likened to language. Various architectural elements such as columns, floors, and windows can be regarded as "vocabulary," and the approaches used to configure them as "grammar." Venturi's architectural rhetoric made use of the framework of human linguistic cognition. After the oil crisis of 1973, a time when Venturi was highly active, the United States saw a rise in construction of housing which made maximal use of solar energy instead of relying on petroleum and other fossil fuel-based power, such as the "solar house" and the "autonomous house." [2] The solar house has south-facing windows occupying as much of the wall as possible, with thermal storage walls inside the windows. The autonomous house features solar panels mounted on an inclined roof sloping to the south. In both these houses, roof and window design is oriented toward harvesting the blessings of nature in the form of solar energy, and in them we see two extremes coexisting: on the one hand treating roof and window elements as "meanings," and on the other, treating them as "objects."

Rather than limiting the scope of Venturi-style combinations to issues of meaning, we aim to expand it to encompass ecosystemic connections among objects and phenomena. This entails organizing architectural elements so they are in mutually beneficial symbiotic relationships.

Our *Row House with Piano Room* (2019), located in a residential area, is a row house that combines a SOHO-type rental unit and a house with a piano lesson room. Local children and adults attend lessons in the piano room, which contains two grand pianos. While

待合室の土間と前庭
Tile-floored waiting room
and front garden

it is a residence, it is partially open to the community, so the piano lesson room's waiting area and the entrance hall are concentrated on the side facing the street, which has continuous rows of aluminum-sash windows. Translucent paper *shoji* screens inside the windows are designed to slide open and closed to as to regulate visibility while admitting light, and at the same time prevent cold or warm air from escaping into the atrium of the entrance hall. Solar water-heating panels are installed on the roof over the entrance hall, which is inclined at approximately 30 degrees, and the collected heat is used for hot water supply and floor heating via a hot-water storage tank. The initial plan was to construct the house entirely with wooden structure, as reinforced concrete construction is more expensive than wood, results in significant CO_2 emissions during the manufacturing process, and is difficult to recycle. However, there is a cliff more than three meters in height at the rear of the site, and as a zoning ordinance requires a protective wall positioned below a 30-degree-angle line from the cliff edge as protection from landslides, the structure employed was a reinforced concrete box with a wooden covering. Concrete was reconsidered not only in light of its structural role, but also as an element that improves the thermal and acoustic environment. In specific terms this meant utilizing concrete's properties as a heat-storing material, with heat from winter sunlight and from the floor heating system accumulating in the concrete frame, and using concrete's mass to enhance the soundproofing of the piano room. The piano room was finished with cedar clapboards to block sound, and glass wool boards and carpet to absorb it. As unfaced concrete makes a hard, cold impression, it was used alongside soft, fine materials such as *shoji* paper, cedar, and wallpaper woven from hemp and pulp, creating the perception

150

of a composite space. Concrete plays the multiple roles of protecting against landslides, utilizing sunlight and heat, and soundproofing the piano room. Meanwhile, the entrance hall windows and the *shoji* screens, the roof inclined at 30 degrees, rainwater collected from the gutters, and watering of plants in the front yard are all interrelated. Things and phenomena including sunlight, rain, the cliff, plants, and sound are organized ecosystemically via elements such as roof, windows, *shoji* screens, and concrete walls. This is an example of an ecosystemic composite of elements.

References

1——Robert Venturi, *Complexity and Contradiction in Architecture*, translated by Ito Kobun, Kajima Institute Publishing, 1982 (original book published 1966).
2——Giovanna Borasi, Mirko Zardini, *Sorry, Out of Gas: Architecture's Response to the 1973 Oil Crisis* (Canadian Center for Architecture, 2007).

上：《ピアノ室のある長屋》
鉄筋コンクリート造と木造
下：コンクリートの壁と障子
Top: Tile-floored waiting room
Reinforced concrete and wood frame
Bottom: Concrete wall and
shoji screens

List of Works

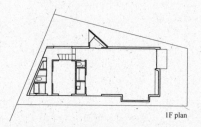

1F plan

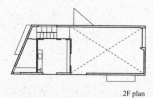

2F plan

section

ホールのある住宅（2009）
敷地面積：217.21㎡／建築面積：108.75㎡
延床面積：149.63㎡／用途：住宅／構造：木造
階数：地上2階／構造設計：オーノJAPAN
施工：広橋工務店

House with Hall, 2009
Site area: 217.21㎡ / Building area: 108.75㎡ / Total floor
area: 149.63㎡ / Use: House / Construction material: Wood
Number of floors: 2 / Structural design: Ohno JAPAN
Builder: Hirohashi Koumuten

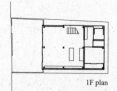

1F plan

2F plan

3F plan

section

Steel House（2012）
敷地面積：94.22㎡／建築面積：43.74㎡
延床面積：70.94㎡／用途：住宅／構造：鉄骨造
階数：地上3階／設計協力：千田友己
構造設計：オーノJAPAN／施工：工藤工務店

Steel House, 2012
Site area: 94.22㎡ / Building area: 43.74㎡ / Total floor
area: 70.94㎡ / Use: House / Construction material: Steel
Number of floors: 3 / Co-designer: Yuki Chida
Structural design: Ohno JAPAN / Builder: Kudo Koumuten

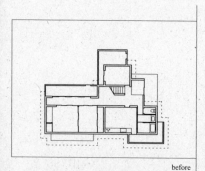

before

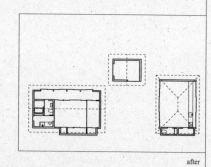

after

高岡のゲストハウス（2016）
敷地面積：462.68㎡／建築面積：90.03㎡
延床面積：90.03㎡／用途：住宅／構造：木造
階数：地上1階／共同設計：能作淳平
構造設計：坂田涼太郎構造設計事務所
施工：モノ・スペース・デザイン、オーデック

Takaoka Guest House, 2016
Site area: 462.68㎡ / Building area: 90.03㎡ / Total floor
area: 90.03㎡ / Use: House / Construction material: Wood
Number of floors: 1 / Co-designer: Junpei Nousaku
Structural design: Ryotaro Sakata Structural Engineers
Builder: MONO SPACE DESIGN, O-dec

1F plan   2F plan   section

馬込の平入（2016）
敷地面積：92.17㎡／建築面積：45.99㎡
延床面積：91.64㎡／用途：住宅／構造：木造
階数：地上2階／構造設計：オーノJAPAN
施工：東京組

Hirairi in Magome, 2016
Site area: 92.17㎡ / Building area: 45.99㎡ / Total floor area: 91.64㎡ / Use: House / Construction material: Wood
Number of floors: 2 / Structural design: Ohno JAPAN
Builder: TOKYO GUMI

赤茶色は改修箇所を示す
Red-brown color indicates sites of renovations

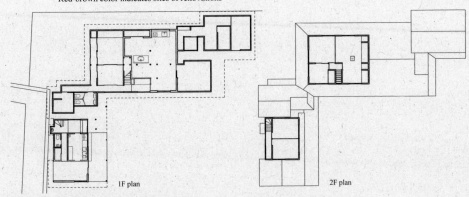

1F plan   2F plan

オチコチ・ヴィレッジ（2016）
敷地面積：834.00㎡／建築面積：142.70㎡
延床面積：186.40㎡／用途：住宅
構造：木造（改修）／階数：地上2階
共同設計：常山未央（Studio mnm）
施工：徳広エネルギー工房

Ochi-Kochi Village, 2016
Site area: 834.00㎡ / Building area: 142.70㎡ / Total floor area: 186.40㎡ / Use: House / Construction material: Wood
(Renovation) / Number of floors: 2
Co-designer: Mio Tsuneyama (Studio mnm)
Builder: Tokuhiro Energy Koubou

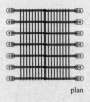

plan   section

Bamboo Theater（2017）
建築面積：81.00㎡／延床面積：81.00㎡
用途：パビリオン／構造：竹造／階数：地上1階
設計協力：Rosario Encarnacion Tan
施工：Rosario Encarnacion Tan
& Avelina Gabat

Bamboo Theater, 2017
Building area: 81.00㎡ / Total floor area: 81.00㎡
Use: Pavilion / Construction material: Bamboo
Number of floors: 1 / Co-designer:
Rosario Encarnacion Tan
Builder: Rosario Encarnacion Tan & Avelina Gabat

1F plan

2F plan

3F plan

4F plan

RF plan

西大井のあな（2017〜）
敷地面積：65.53㎡／建築面積：42.74㎡
延床面積：151.17㎡／用途：住宅＋事務所
構造：鉄骨造／階数：地上4階
共同設計：常山未央（Studio mnm）
施工：工藤工務店＋team nishiooi（自主施工）

Holes in the House (Casa A Nishioi), 2017–
Site area: 65.53㎡ / Building area: 42.74㎡ / Total floor
area: 151.17㎡ / Use: House + office / Construction
material: Steel / Number of floors: 4
Co-design: Mio Tsuneyama (Studio mnm)
Builder: Kudo Koumuten + team nishiooi (Self-build)

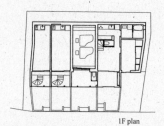
1F plan

2F plan

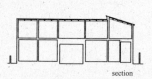
section

ピアノ室のある長屋（2018）
敷地面積：221.21㎡／建築面積：123.83㎡
延床面積：228.33㎡／用途：長屋
構造：木造＋RC造／階数：地上1階
構造設計：オーノJAPAN
設備設計：ZO設計室／施工：工藤工務店

Row House with Piano Room, 2018
Site area: 221.21㎡ / Building area: 123.83㎡ / Total floor
area: 228.33㎡ / Use: Row House / Construction material:
Wood + RC / Number of floors: 1 / Structural design:
Ohno JAPAN / Facility design: Zo Consulting Engineers
Builder: Kudo Komuten

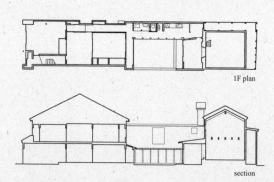
1F plan

section

山町筋の町家改修（2019計画案）
敷地面積：236.29㎡／建築面積：160.46㎡
延床面積：278.34㎡／用途：住宅
構造：木造（改修）／階数：地上2階

Machiya Renovation in Yamachosuji, 2019 (Plan)
Site area: 236.29㎡ / Building area: 160.46㎡ / Total floor
area: 278.34㎡ / Use: House / Construction material:
Wood (Renovation) / Number of floors: 2

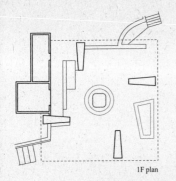

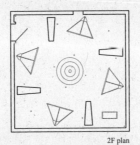

1F plan

2F plan

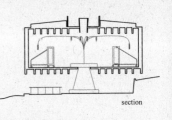

section

Cosmo-Eggs（2019）
ヴェネチア・ビエンナーレ日本館
建築面積：241.65㎡／延床面積：508.76㎡
用途：展示会場／構造：RC造
階数：地上2階／展示制作：下道基行、
安野太郎、石倉敏明、能作文徳
グラフィックデザイン：田中義久／施工：ヒグレ

Cosmo-Eggs, 2019
The Japan Pavilion Venice Biennale
Building area: 241.65㎡ / Total floor area: 508.76㎡
Use: Exhibition hall / Construction material: RC
Number of floors: 2 / Exhibition production:
Motoyuki Shitamichi, Taro Yasuno, Toshiaki Ishikura,
Fuminori Nousaku / Graphic design: Yoshihisa Tanaka
Builder: HIGURE

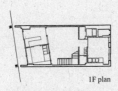

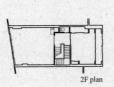

1F plan

2F plan

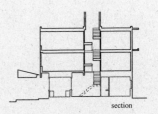

section

考えるパンKOPPE（2020）
敷地面積：169.14㎡／建築面積：65.30㎡
延床面積：203.71㎡／用途：店舗＋住宅
構造：RC造（改修）／階数：地上3階
施工：建協

Kangaeru Pan Koppe (Thinking Bread Koppe), 2020
Site area: 169.14㎡ / Building area: 65.30㎡ / Total floor
area: 203.71㎡ / Use: Shop + House / Construction
material: RC (Renovation) / Number of floors: 3
Builder: Kenkyo Co., Ltd.

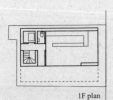

1F plan

3F plan

5F plan

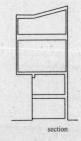

section

蔵前の写真スタジオ（2020計画案）
敷地面積：100.03㎡／建築面積：69.73㎡
延床面積：209.90㎡／用途：店舗＋オフィス
構造：木造＋RC造／階数：地上5階

Photo Studio in Kuramae, 2020 (Plan)
Site area: 100.03㎡ / Building area: 69.73㎡ / Total floor
area: 209.90㎡ / Use: Shop + Office / Construction
material: Wood + RC / Number of floors: 5

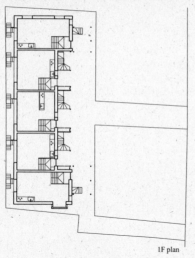

1F plan

2F plan

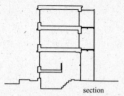

section

コーポラティブハウス用賀（2020計画案）
敷地面積：365.97㎡／建築面積：210.10㎡
延床面積：711.14㎡／用途：集合住宅
構造：RC造／階数：地下1階＋地上3階
共同設計：常山未央（Studio mnm）、
齋藤由和（アデザイン）
構造設計：オーノJAPAN

Cooperative House Youga, 2020 (Plan)
Site area: 365.97㎡ / Building area: 210.10㎡
Total floor area: 711.14㎡ / Use: Housing complex
Construction material: RC / Number of floors:
1 basement, 3 aboveground / Co-design: Mio Tsuneyama
(Studio mnm), Yuwa Saitou (a design inc.)
Structural design: Ohno JAPAN

1F plan

2F plan

3F plan

section

荏原中延の住宅（2020計画案）
敷地面積：58.14㎡／建築面積：24.95㎡
延床面積：64.70㎡／用途：住宅／構造：木造
階数：地上3階
共同設計：常山未央（Studio mnm）

House in Ebaranakanobu, 2020 (Plan)
Site area: 58.14㎡ / Building area: 24.95㎡
Total floor area: 64.70㎡ / Use: House
Construction material: Wood / Number of floors: 3
Co-design: Mio Tsuneyama (Studio mnm)

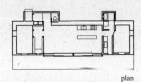

plan   section

明野の高床（2021）
敷地面積：829.28㎡／建築面積：135.76㎡
延床面積：78.34㎡／用途：住宅／構造：木造
階数：地上1階／構造設計：オーノJAPAN
施工：小澤建築工房、
日本ストローベイルハウス研究会

Akeno Raised-Floor House, 2021
Site area: 829.28㎡ / Building area: 135.76㎡ / Total floor
area: 78.34㎡ / Use: House / Construction material: Wood
Number of floors: 1 / Structural design: Ohno JAPAN
Builder: Ozawa Standard, Japan Straw Bale House
Association

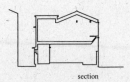

1F plan   2F plan   section

東尾久のスタジオ（2021）
敷地面積：50.03㎡／建築面積：36.21㎡
延床面積：70.33㎡／用途：住宅／構造：木造
階数：地上2階／構造設計：オーノJAPAN
施工：工藤工務店

Studio in Higashi-Ogu, 2021
Site area: 50.03㎡ / Building area: 36.21㎡ / Total floor
area: 70.33㎡ / Use: House / Construction material: Wood
Number of floors: 2 / Structural design: Ohno JAPAN
Builder: Kudo Koumuten

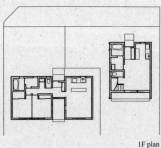

site plan   1F plan

section

氷見移住ヴィレッジ（2021）
敷地面積：514.85㎡（1730.85㎡）
建築面積：99.35㎡／延床面積：121.69㎡
用途：住宅／構造：木造／階数：地上1階＋2階
共同設計：常山未央、東工業／施工：東工業

Himi Migrant Village, 2021
Site area: 514.85㎡ (1730.85㎡) / Building area: 99.35㎡
Total floor area: 121.69㎡ / Use: House
Construction material: Wood / Number of floors: 1 / 2
Co-designer: Mio Tsuneyama (Studio mnm), Azuma Kogyo
Builder: Azuma Kogyo

能作文徳

1982年　富山県生まれ
2005年　東京工業大学工学部建築学科卒業
2007年　東京工業大学大学院理工学研究科建築学専攻修士課程修了
2008年　Njiric+Arhitekti（クロアチア）海外研修
2010年　能作文徳建築設計事務所設立
2012年　博士（工学）学位取得（東京工業大学）
2012-18年　東京工業大学大学院環境・社会理工学院建築学系助教
2018年-　東京電機大学未来科学部建築学科准教授

受賞歴

平成22年東京建築士会住宅建築賞《ホールのある住宅》、SDレビュー2013鹿島賞《高岡のゲストハウス》（能作淳平と共同設計）、第15回ヴェネチア・ビエンナーレ国際建築展日本館展示特別表彰（en[縁]：アート・オブ・ネクサス）、SDレビュー2017入選《西大井のあな》（常山未央と共同設計）、ISAIA2018 Excellent Research Award《西大井のあな》、第58回ヴェネチア・ビエンナーレ国際美術展日本館展示出展《Cosmo-Eggs｜宇宙の卵》、建築設計学会Architects of the year 2019入選《西大井のあな》、住まいの環境デザインアワード2020優秀賞《ピアノ室のある長屋》、gallery IHA住宅建築賞《明野の高床》。

著書

『WindowScape 窓のふるまい学』（共著、フィルムアート、2010）、『WindowScape 2 窓と街並の系譜学』（共著、フィルムアート、2014）、『アトリエ・ワン コモナリティーズ』（共著、LIXIL出版、2014）、『シェアの思想──または愛と制度と空間の関係』（共著、LIXIL出版、2015）、『WindowScape 3 窓の仕事学』（共著、フィルムアート、2017）、『共感・時間・建築』（共著、TOTO出版、2019）、『Cosmo-Eggs｜宇宙の卵』（共著、LIXIL出版／Case Publishing、2019）、『Cosmo-Eggs｜宇宙の卵──コレクティブ以降のアート』（共著、torch press、2020）。

協力

Studio mnm（常山未央）
ノウサクジュンペイアーキテクツ（能作淳平）
能作文徳建築設計事務所
（所員：水上俊也、土屋瑛衣子
元所員：澤田航、大田美奈子、近藤有希子、中山陽介）
東京電機大学能作研究室

Fuminori Nousaku

1982   Born in Toyama, Japan
2005   Bachelor Degree in Architecture from Tokyo Institute of Technology
2007   Master Degree in Architecture from Tokyo Institute of Technology
2008   Trained overseas at Njiric + Arhitekti (Croatia)
2010   Established Fuminori Nousaku Architects
2012   Doctorate in Engineering from Tokyo Institute of Technology
2012–18   Assistant Professor of Architecture, Tokyo Institute of Technology
School of Environment and Society
2018–   Associate Professor of Architecture, Tokyo Denki University School
of Science and Technology for Future Life

Awards

2010 Tokyo Residential Architecture Prize (*House with Hall*), 2013 SD Review Kajima Prize (*Guest House in Takaoka*) (co-designed with Junpei Nousaku), 2016 Special Mention, Japan Pavilion at Venice Biennale 15th International Architecture Exhibition (*en: art of nexus*), 2017 SD Review Prize (*Holes in the House [Casa A Nishioi]*) (co-designed with Mio Tsuneyama), ISAIA2018 Excellent Research Award (*Holes in the House [Casa A Nishioi]*), 2019 Japan Pavilion at 58th Venice Biennale International Art Exhibition (*Cosmo-Eggs* exhibit), 2019 Architects of the Year (*Holes in the House [Casa A Nishioi]*), 2020 Environment-Friendly Home Awards (*Row House with Piano Room*), 2020 Gallery IHA Residential Architecture Award (*Akeno Raised-Floor House*)

Books

WindowScape: Window Behaviorology (co-author, Film Art, 2010), *WindowScape 2: Window and Cityscape Genealogy* (co-author, Film Art, 2014), *Atelier Bow Wow: Commonalities* (co-author, LIXIL Publishing, 2014), *The "Share" Mentality — Or the Relationality of Love, Systems and Spaces* (co-author, LIXIL Publishing, 2015), *WindowScape 3: Window Workology* (co-author, Film Art, 2017), *Empathy, Time, Architecture* (co-author, TOTO Publishing, 2019), *Cosmo-Eggs* (co-author, LIXIL Publishing / Case Publishing, 2019), *Cosmo-Eggs: Reflections on Cosmo-Eggs at the Japan Pavilion at La Biennale di Venezia 2019* (co-author, torch press, 2020).

Special thanks to:

Studio mnm (Mio Tsuneyama)
Junpei Nousaku Architects (Junpei Nousaku)
Fuminori Nousaku Architects
(Members: Toshiya Mizugami, Eiko Tsuchiya
Past Members: Wataru Sawada, Minako Ota,
Yukiko Kondo, Yosuke Nakayama)
Fuminori Nousaku Laboratory, Tokyo Denki University

撮影／Photo

- 鈴木淳平／Jumpei Suzuki
  pp.040, 068, 069, 070, 071, 074（上下／Above, Bottom）, 078, 079, 096-097,
  098, 099（下／Bottom）, 100, 101, 102, 110-111, 113, 118, 125（左／Left）,
  142, 143, 148（左右／Left, Right）, 150, 151（下／Bottom）
- 新建築社写真部／Shinkenchiku-sha
  pp.043, 048, 099（上／Above）
- 歌津亮悟／Ryogo Utatsu
  pp.044, 045, 049, 053, 054
- アーカイ美味んぐ／ArchiBIMIng
  提供＝国際交流基金／Courtesy of the Japan Foundation
  pp.073, 076
  提供＝国際交流基金／Courtesy of the Japan Foundation
  p.088（左右／Left, Right）
- 津田直／Nao Tsuda
  pp.131（左右／Left, Right）
- 能作文徳建築設計事務所／Fuminori Nousaku Architects
  pp.004-005, 047, 057, 066, 067, 081, 082, 104（左右／Left, Right）,
  105, 106（左右／Left, Right）, 107, 108（左右／Left, Right）, 114,
  121（左右／Left, Right）, 122（左右／Left, Right）, 123（左右／Left, Right）,
  125（右／Right）, 126（左右／Left, Right）, 129, 137（左右／Left, Right）,
  139, 140（左右／Left, Right）, 151（上／Above）

作成／illustration

- オーノJAPAN／Ohno JAPAN
  p.115
- 東京電機大学能作研究室／
  Fuminori Nousaku Laboratory, Tokyo Denki University
  pp.138, 141
- 能作文徳建築設計事務所／Fuminori Nousaku Architects
  pp.050-051, 060, 084, 085, 093, 112, 116-117, 132, 146-147

現代建築家コンセプト・シリーズ 29
能作文徳｜野生のエディフィス

発行日：2021年2月15日 初版第1刷発行
著者：能作文徳
発行者：ジン・ソン・モンテサーノ
発行所：LIXIL出版
〒136-8535 東京都江東区大島2-1-1
TEL. 03-3638-8021　FAX. 03-3638-8022
https://livingculture.lixil.com/publish/

企画・編集：飯尾次郎、中村睦美（スペルプラーツ）
翻訳：クリストファー・スティヴンズ
デザイン：田中義久、山田悠太朗
シリーズ・デザイン：マッチアンドカンパニー
印刷：株式会社加藤文明社

ISBN978-4-86480-052-5 C0352